Barefoot in the Park

BAREFOOT

A New Comedy by

IN THE PARK

NEIL SIMON

Random House
New York

897

Photographs by courtesy of Friedman-Abeles

BAREFOOT IN THE PARK *was first presented by Saint Subber at the Biltmore Theatre, New York City, N.Y., on October 23, 1963, with the following cast:*

CORIE BRATTER	Elizabeth Ashley
TELEPHONE MAN	Herbert Edelman
DELIVERY MAN	Joseph Keating
PAUL BRATTER	Robert Redford
MRS. BANKS	Mildred Natwick
VICTOR VELASCO	Kurt Kasznar

Directed by Mike Nichols

Setting by Oliver Smith

Lighting by Jean Rosenthal

Costumes by Donald Brooks

The entire action of the play takes place in the top-floor apartment in a brownstone on East Forty-eighth Street, New York City.

Act One

About 5:30 on a cold February afternoon.

Act Two

Scene 1. Four days later, about 7:00 P.M.
Scene 2. Later that night, about 2:00 A.M.

Act Three

The following day, about 5:00 P.M.

Act One

ACT ONE

A large one-room apartment on the top floor of an old brownstone on East Forty-eighth Street off Third Avenue. The room is barren. A ladder, a canvas drop cloth, and a couple of empty paint cans stand forlornly in the center of the room. There is a huge skylight which pours the bright February sunshine glaringly into the room. Through the skylight we can see the roofs and windows of brownstones across the street and the framework of a large building under construction. Crests of clinging snow can be seen in the two windows under the skylight. At stage right, there is the entrance door, a step below the apartment itself. At stage left, four steps lead to a raised area from which two doors open, the upstage one leading to a bathroom, the other to the bedroom. We will soon learn that the latter is not really a bedroom, but a small dressing room. The bathroom has only a shower and a sink and what-have-you. On another raised section up right is the kitchen. It's not really a kitchen, but just an old stove, an older refrigerator, and a chipped sink standing nakedly between them. Upstage left of this area is another platform on which stand a steamer trunk and a few suitcases. The room has just been freshly painted—not carefully, maybe not professionally, but painted. There is a small Franklin stove downstage left below the platform, and an open closet downstage right. Completing the furnishings of the room are a railing that runs downstage of the entrance wall, and a radiator that sits high on the upstage left wall. For all the room's drabness and coldness, there is great promise here. Someone with taste, imagination, and personality can make this that

3

perfect love nest we all dream about. That person is now putting the key in the door.

It opens and CORIE BRATTER *enters. She is lovely, young, and full of hope for the future. She enters the apartment, looks around, and sighs as though the world were just beginning. For her, it is. She is wearing Levis and a yellow top under a large, shaggy white fur coat; she carries a bouquet of flowers. After rapturously examining the room, she takes the small paint can, fills it with water, and puts in the flowers, throwing the wrapping on the floor. The first bit of color in the room. As she crosses to put the "vase" on top of the Franklin stove, the doorbell buzzes. She puts the flowers down, crosses to the door, buzzes back, and then opens the door and shouts down:*

CORIE   Hello?
> (*From the depths, possibly from the bottom of the earth we hear a voice shout up*)

VOICE   Bratter?

CORIE (*Yelling back*)   Yes. Up here! . . . Top floor!
> (*She crosses to the suitcases, opens the medium-sized one and takes out a large bottle of champagne which she puts into the refrigerator*)

VOICE (*From below, this time a little closer*)   Hello?

CORIE (*Rushes to the door again and shouts down*)   Up here! You have another floor to go.
> (*Crossing back to the open suitcase she takes out three small logs and carries them to the Franklin stove. As she drops them in front of the stove, the owner of the voice appears at the door: a tall, heavy-set man in his mid-thirties, in a plaid wool jacket and baseball cap. He is breathing very, very hard*)

TELEPHONE MAN Tel—(*He tries to catch his breath*)— Telephone Company.

CORIE Oh, the phone. Good. Come on in.
(*He steps in, carrying a black leather repair kit*)

TELEPHONE MAN That's quite a—(*Gasp, gasp*)—quite a climb.

CORIE Yes, it's five flights. If you don't count the front stoop.

TELEPHONE MAN I *counted* the front stoop. (*Gasp, gasp . . . he looks at his notebook*) Paul Bratter, right?

CORIE *Mrs.* Paul Bratter.

TELEPHONE MAN (*Still checking the book*) Princess phone?

CORIE The little one? That lights up? In beige?

TELEPHONE MAN The little one . . . (*Gasp, gasp*) That lights up . . . (*Gasp, gasp*) In beige . . . (*Gasp, gasp. He swallows hard*)

CORIE Would you like a glass of water?

TELEPHONE MAN (*Sucking for air, nods*) Please!

CORIE (*Crosses to the sink*) I'd offer you soda or a beer but we don't have anything yet.

TELEPHONE MAN A glass of water's fine.

5

CORIE (*Suddenly embarrassed*) Except I don't have a glass either.

TELEPHONE MAN Oh!

CORIE Nothing's arrived yet . . . You could put your head under and just schlurp.

TELEPHONE MAN No, I'm okay. Just a little out of shape. (*As he climbs stiffly up the step out of the well, he groans with pain. After looking about*) Where do you want the phone?

CORIE (*Looks around*) The phone . . . Let me see . . . Gee, I don't know. Do you have any ideas?

TELEPHONE MAN Well, it depends what you're gonna do with the room. You gonna have furniture in here?

CORIE Yes, it's on its way up.

TELEPHONE MAN (*He looks back at the stairs*) *Heavy* furniture?

CORIE I'll tell you what. (*She points to the telephone junction box on the wall left of the stairs*) Just put it over there and give me a long extension cord. If I can't find a place, I'll just hang it out the window.

TELEPHONE MAN Fair enough. (*He crosses to the junction box, coughing and in pain*) Whoo!

CORIE Say, I'm awfully sorry about the stairs.
(*Taking the large suitcase, she starts to drag it into the bedroom*)

TELEPHONE MAN (*On his knees; he opens his tool box*) You're really gonna live up here, heh? . . . I mean, every day?

CORIE Every day.

TELEPHONE MAN You don't mind it?

CORIE (*Stopping on the stairs*) Mind it? . . . I love this apartment . . . besides (*she continues into the bedroom*) it *does* discourage people.

TELEPHONE MAN What people?

CORIE (*Comes out of the bedroom and starts for the other suitcases*) Mothers, friends, relatives, mothers. I mean no one just pops in on you when they have to climb five flights.

TELEPHONE MAN You're a newlywed, right?

CORIE Six days. What gave me away?

TELEPHONE MAN I watch "What's My Line" a lot.
    (*The doorbell buzzes*)

CORIE Oh! I hope that's the furniture.

TELEPHONE MAN I don't want to see this.

CORIE (*Presses the buzzer and yells down the stairs*) Helloooo! Bloomingdale's?
    (*From below, a voice*)

VOICE Lord and Taylor.

CORIE Lord and Taylor? (*Shrugs and takes the now empty suitcase and puts it into the closet*) Probably another wedding gift . . . From my mother. She sends me wedding gifts twice a day . . .

TELEPHONE MAN I hope it's an electric heater.
(*He blows on his hands*)

CORIE (*Worried, she feels the steam pipe next to the closet*) Really? Is it cold in here?

TELEPHONE MAN I can't grip the screwdriver. Maybe the steam is off.

CORIE Maybe that's it.
(*She gets up on the stairs and tests the radiator*)

TELEPHONE MAN Just turn it on. It'll come right up.

CORIE It *is* on. It's just not coming up.

TELEPHONE MAN Oh! . . . Well, that's these old brownstones for you.
(*He zips up his jacket*)

CORIE I prefer it this way. It's a medical fact, you know, that steam heat is very bad for you.

TELEPHONE MAN Yeah? In February?
(*Suddenly the DELIVERY MAN appears in the door, carrying three packages. He is in his early sixties and from the way he is breathing, it seems the end is very near. He gasps for air*)

CORIE (*Crossing to him*) Oh, hi . . . Just put it down
. . . anywhere.
(*The* DELIVERY MAN *puts the packages down,
panting. He wants to talk but can't. He extends his
hand to the* TELEPHONE MAN *for a bit of compassion*)

TELEPHONE MAN I know. I know.

CORIE I'm awfully sorry about the stairs. (*The* DELIVERY
MAN *takes out a pad and pencil and holds them out
limply toward* CORIE) What's this?

TELEPHONE MAN I think he wants you to sign it.

CORIE Oh, yes. (*She signs it quickly*) Wait, just a minute.
(*She picks up her bag from where she had left it in the
kitchen area and takes out some change*) Here you go
. . . (*She puts it in his hand. He nods weakly and
turns to go*) Will you be all right? . . . (*And for the
first time he gets out some words. They are: "Argh,
argh." He exits*)

CORIE (*Closes the door behind him*) It's a shame, isn't
it? Giving such hard work to an old man.
(*She takes two of the packages and puts them with
the remaining suitcases*)

TELEPHONE MAN He's probably only twenty-five. They
age fast on this route. (*He dials the phone and then talks
into it*) Hello, Ed? Yeah . . . On . . . er . . . Eldorado
five, eight, one, nine, one . . . Give me a straight check.

CORIE (*Moving to* TELEPHONE MAN) Is that my number? Eldorado five, eight, one, nine, one (*The* TELE-
PHONE MAN *nods*) It has a nice sound, hasn't it?

9

TELEPHONE MAN (*Why fool with a romantic*) Yeah, it's a beautiful number. (*The phone rings. He answers it, disguising his voice*) Hello? . . . (*He chuckles over his joke*) Good work, Mr. Bell, you've done it again. (*He hangs up, and turns to* CORIE) Well, you've got your phone. As my mother would say, may your first call be from the Sweepstakes.

CORIE (*Takes the phone*) My very own phone . . . Gives you a sense of power, doesn't it? Can I make a call yet?

TELEPHONE MAN (*Putting the cover back on the junction box*) Your bill started two minutes ago.

CORIE Who can I call? . . . I know.
(*She starts to dial*)

TELEPHONE MAN Oh, by the way. My name is Harry Pepper. And if you ever have any trouble with this phone, please, do me a favor, don't ask for Harry Pepper. (CORIE *hangs up, a look of disappointment on her face*) What's the matter, bad news?

CORIE (*Like a telephone operator*) It is going to be cloudy tonight with a light snow.

TELEPHONE MAN (*He looks up at the skylight*) And just think, you'll be the first one in the city to see it fall.
(*The doorbell buzzes.* CORIE *puts down the phone, and rushes to the door*)

CORIE Oh, please, let that be the furniture and not Paul so Paul can see the apartment with furniture. (*She buzzes, opens the door, and yells downstairs*) Yes?

VOICE FROM BELOW It's me!

CORIE (*Unhappily*) Oh, hi, Paul. (*She turns into the room*) Well, I guess he sees the apartment without the furniture.
(*She takes the remaining package and places it with the others on the landing under the windows*)

TELEPHONE MAN (*Gathering up his tools*) How long d'ja say you were married?

CORIE Six days.

TELEPHONE MAN He won't notice the place is empty until June. (*He crosses to the door*) Well, Eldorado five, eight, one, nine, one . . . Have a nice marriage . . . (*He turns back into the room*) And may you soon have many extensions. (*He turns and looks at the climb down he has to make and moans*) Ooohh!
(*He is gone.* CORIE *quickly starts to prepare the room for* PAUL'*s entrance. She gathers up the canvas drop cloth and throws it into the closet*)

PAUL'S VOICE Corie? . . . Where are you?

CORIE (*Rushes back to the door and yells down*) Up here, hon . . . Top floor . . . (*The phone rings*) Oh, my goodness. The phone. (*She rushes to it and answers it*) Hello? . . . Yes? . . . Oh, yes, he is . . . I mean he's on his way up . . . Can you hold on for two more floors? (*She puts down the receiver and yells*) Paul. Hurry up, darling!

PAUL'S VOICE Okay. Okay.

CORIE (*Into the phone*) Hello. He'll be with you in one more flight. Thank you. (*She puts the phone on the floor and continues to get the apartment ready. Rushing up the stairs, she closes the bedroom and bathroom doors. Surveying the room, she sees the wrapping from the flowers on the floor of the kitchen and the wadded-up newspapers on top of the stove. Quickly gathering them up, she stuffs them into the nearest hiding place—the refrigerator. Then dashing into the hall and closing the door behind her, she re-enters to make one more survey of her apartment. Satisfied with what she sees, she turns back to the open door, and yells down*) Now honey, don't expect too much. The furniture didn't get here yet and the paint didn't come out exactly right, but I think it's going to be beautiful . . . Paul? . . . Paul, are you all right?

PAUL'S VOICE I'm coming. I'm coming.

CORIE (*Runs back to the phone and speaks into it*) He's coming. He's coming. (*She puts down the phone and looks at the door.* PAUL *falls in through the doorway and hangs on the rail at the entrance to the apartment.* PAUL *is twenty-six but breathes and dresses like fifty-six. He carries a heavy suitcase and an attaché case and all the dignity he can bear. He drops the attaché case at the railing*) Hi, sweetheart. (*She smothers him with kisses but all he can do is fight for air*) . . . Oh, Paul, darling. (PAUL *sucks for oxygen*) . . . Well? (*She steps back*) Say something.

PAUL (*Breathing with great difficulty, he looks back down the stairs*) It's six flights . . . Did you know it's six flights?

CORIE It isn't. It's five.

PAUL (*Staggers up the step into the room, and collapses on the suitcase*) What about that big thing hanging outside the building?

CORIE That's not a flight. It's a stoop.

PAUL It may *look* like a stoop but it climbs like a flight. (*Gasp, gasp*)

CORIE Is that *all* you have to say?

PAUL (*Gasping*) I didn't think I'd get that much out. (*He breathes heavily*) It didn't seem like six flights when I first saw the apartment. (*Gasp*) Why is that?

CORIE You didn't see the apartment. Don't you remember, the woman wasn't home. You saw the third-floor apartment.

PAUL Then that's why.

CORIE (*Crossing above* PAUL) You don't like it. You really don't like it.

PAUL I *do* like it. (*He squints around*) I'm just waiting for my eyes to clear first.

CORIE I expected you to walk in here and say, "Wow." (*She takes his hand*)

PAUL I will. (*He takes a deep breath*) Okay. (*He looks around, then says without enthusiasm*) "Wow."

CORIE Oh, Paul. (*She throws herself onto* PAUL's *knee*)

13

It'll be beautiful, I promise you. You just came home too soon.

(*She nuzzles him*)

PAUL   You know I missed you.

CORIE   Did you really?

PAUL   Right in the middle of the Monday morning conference I began to feel sexy.

CORIE   That's marvelous. (*They kiss*) Oh, boy. Let's take a cab back to the Plaza. We still have an hour before check-out time.

PAUL   We can't. We took a towel and two ash trays. We're hot.

(*He kisses her*)

CORIE   My gosh, you still love me.

PAUL   After six days at the Plaza? What's the trick?

CORIE (*Gets up and moves away*)   But that was a honeymoon. Now we're on a regular schedule. I thought you'd come home tonight, and we'd shake hands and start the marriage.

(*She extends her hand to him*)

PAUL (*Rises*)   "How do you do? . . ."

(*They shake hands. Then* CORIE *throws herself into his arms and kisses him*)

CORIE   My turn to say "Wow" . . . For a lawyer you're some good kisser.

PAUL (*With hidden import*) For a kisser I'm some good lawyer.

CORIE What does that mean? . . . Something's happened? . . . Something wonderful? . . . Well, for pete's sakes, what?

PAUL It's not positive yet. The office is supposed to call and let me know in five minutes.

CORIE (*Then she remembers*) Oh! They called!

PAUL What . . . ?

CORIE I mean they're calling.

PAUL When . . . ?

CORIE Now . . . They're on the phone now.

PAUL (*Looking around*) Where . . . ?

CORIE (*Points to the phone*) There . . .

PAUL (*Rushes to the phone*) Why didn't you tell me?

CORIE I forgot. You kissed me and got me all crazy.

PAUL (*Into the phone*) Frank? . . . Yeah! . . . Listen, what did—oh, very funny. (*Looks to* CORIE) "For a lawyer, I'm some good kisser" . . . Come on, come, tell me? . . . Well? . . . (*A big grin.* CORIE *feeling left out, sneaks over and tries to tickle him*) You're kidding? The whole thing? Oh, Frank, baby. I love you . . . What do you mean, nervous? . . . I passed the bar, didn't I? . . .

Yes, I'll go over everything tonight. (CORIE *reacts to "tonight" and slowly moves to the ladder*) I'll meet you in Schrafft's at eight o'clock in the morning. We'll go over the briefs . . . Hey, what kind of a tie do I wear? I don't know. I thought maybe something flowing like Oliver Wendell Holmes . . . Right. (*He stands up. He is bubbling with joy.* CORIE *has now climbed up the ladder*) Did you hear? . . . Did you hear?
(*He moves up the ladder to* CORIE)

CORIE   What about tonight?

PAUL   I've got to be in court tomorrow morning . . . *I've got my first case!*

CORIE   What about tonight?

PAUL   I'll have to go over the briefs. Marshall has to be in Washington tomorrow and he wants me to take over . . . with Frank . . . but it's really my case. (*He hugs* CORIE) Oh, Corie, baby, I'm going to be a lawyer.

CORIE   That's wonderful . . . I just thought we were going to spend tonight together.

PAUL   We'll spend tomorrow night together. (*He crosses to railing and gets his attaché case*) I hope I brought those affidavits.

CORIE   *I brought a black lace nightgown.*
(*She crosses to the small suitcase*)

PAUL   (*Looks through affidavits from the case; his mind has now turned completely legal*) Marshall had everything laid out when I was at the office . . . It looks simple enough. A furrier is suing a woman for nonpayment of bills.

CORIE (*Taking the nightgown out of the suitcase*)   I was going to cook you spaghetti with the white clam sauce . . . in a bikini.

PAUL   We're representing the furrier. He made four specially tailored coats for this woman on Park Avenue. Now she doesn't want the coats.

CORIE (*Takes off her sweatshirt, and slipping her arms through the nightgown straps, she drapes it over her*) Then I found this great thing on Eighth Street. It's a crossword puzzle with dirty words.

PAUL   But the furrier can't get rid of the coats. She's only four-foot-eight. He'd have to sell them to a rich little girl.

CORIE   . . . then I was going to put on a record and do an authentic Cambodian fertility dance.

PAUL   The only trouble is, he didn't have a signed contract . . . (CORIE *begins her "fertility dance" and ends up collapsing on the bottom step of the ladder*) What are you doing?

CORIE   I'm trying to get you all hot and bothered and you're summing up for the jury. The whole marriage is over.

PAUL (*Moves to* CORIE)   Oh, Corie, honey, I'm sorry. (*He puts his arms around her*) I guess I'm pretty excited. You want me to be rich and famous, don't you?

CORIE   During the day. At night I want you to be here and sexy.

PAUL   I will. Just as soon as Birnbaum versus Gump is over . . . I'll tell you what. Tomorrow night is your night. We'll do whatever you want.

CORIE   Something wild, insane, and crazy?

PAUL   I promise.

CORIE (*Her eyes wide open*)   Like what?

PAUL   Well . . . I'll come home early and we'll wallpaper each other.

CORIE   Oh, Paul, how wonderful . . . Can't we do it to-night?

PAUL   No, we can't do it tonight, because tonight I've got to work. (*He rises, and looks around*) Except where do I sit?

CORIE   The furniture will be here by five. They promised.

PAUL (*Drops the affidavits into the attaché case, and looks at his watch*)   Five? . . . It's five-thirty. (*He crosses to the bedroom stairs*) What do we do, sleep in Bloomingdale's tonight?

CORIE   They'll be here, Paul. They're probably stuck in traffic.

PAUL (*Crossing up to the bedroom*)   And what about tonight? I've got a case in court tomorrow. Maybe we should check into a hotel?

(*He looks into the bedroom*)

CORIE (*Rises and moves toward* PAUL) We just checked *out* of a hotel. I don't care if the furniture *doesn't* come. I'm sleeping in my apartment *tonight*.

PAUL Where? Where? (*He looks into the bathroom, closes the door, and starts to come back down the steps*) There's only room for *one* in the bathtub. (*He suddenly turns, goes back up the steps and opens the door to the bathroom*) Where's the bathtub?

CORIE (*Hesitantly*) There is no bathtub.

PAUL No bathtub?

CORIE There's a shower . . .

PAUL How am I going to take a bath?

CORIE You won't take a bath. You'll take a shower.

PAUL I don't like showers. I like baths. Corie, how am I going to take a bath?

CORIE You'll lie down in the shower and hang your feet over the sink . . . I'm sorry there's no bathtub, Paul.

PAUL (*Closes the door, and crosses down into the room*) Hmmmm . . . Boy, of all the nights . . . (*He suddenly shivers*) It's freezing in here. (*He rubs his hands*) Isn't there any heat?

CORIE Of course there's heat. We have a radiator.

PAUL (*Gets up on the steps and feels the radiator*) The *radiator's* the coldest thing in the room.

CORIE It's probably the boiler. It's probably off in the whole building.

PAUL (*Putting on his gloves*) No, it was warm coming up the stairs. (*He goes out the door into the hall*) See . . . It's nice and warm out here.

CORIE Maybe it's because the apartment is empty.

PAUL The *hall* is empty too, but it's warm out here.

CORIE (*Moves to the stove*) It'll be all right once I get a fire going.

PAUL (*Goes to the phone*) A fire? You'd have to keep the flame going night and day . . . I'll call the landlord.

CORIE (*Putting a log into the stove*) He's not home.

PAUL Where is he?

CORIE In Florida! . . . There's a handyman that comes Monday, Wednesday, and Fridays.

PAUL You mean we freeze on Tuesdays, Thursdays, and Saturdays?

CORIE He'll be here in the morning.

PAUL (*Moving to the windows*) And what'll we do to-night? I've got a case in court in the morning.

CORIE (*Moves to* PAUL) Will you stop saying it like you always have a case in court in the morning. This is your first one.

PAUL Well, what'll we do?

CORIE The furniture will be here. In the meantime I can light the stove and you can sit over the fire with your law books and a shawl like Abraham Lincoln.
(*She crosses to the Franklin stove and gets matches from the top of it*)

PAUL Is that supposed to be funny?
(*He begins to investigate the small windows*)

CORIE No. It was supposed to be nasty. It just came out funny. (*She strikes a match and attempts to light the log in the stove.* PAUL *tries the windows*) What are you doing?
(*She gives up attempting to light the log*)

PAUL I'm checking to see if the windows are closed.

CORIE They're closed. I looked.

PAUL Then why is it windy in here?

CORIE (*Moves toward* PAUL) I don't feel a draft.

PAUL (*Moves away from the windows*) I didn't say draft. I said wind . . . There's a brisk northeasterly wind blowing in this room.

CORIE You don't have to get sarcastic.

PAUL (*Moving up into the kitchen area*) I'm not getting sarcastic, I'm getting chapped lips. (*Looking up, he glimpses the hole in the skylight*)

CORIE How could there be wind in a closed room?

PAUL How's this for an answer? There's a hole in the skylight.
(*He points up*)

CORIE (*Looks up, sees it, and is obviously embarrassed by it*) Gee, I didn't see that before. Did you?

PAUL (*Moves to the ladder*) I didn't see the *apartment* before.

CORIE (*Defensively. She crosses to the railing and gets her coat*) All right, Paul, don't get upset. I'm sure it'll be fixed. We could plug it up with something for tonight.

PAUL (*Gets up on the ladder*) How? How? That's twenty feet high. You'd have to fly over in a plane and *drop* something in.

CORIE (*Putting on her coat*) It's only for one night. And it's not that cold.

PAUL In February? Do you know what it's like at three o'clock in the morning? In February? Ice-cold freezing.

CORIE It's not going to be freezing. I called the Weather Bureau. It's going to be cloudy with a light s—
(*She catches herself and looks up*)

PAUL   What? (CORIE *turns away*) What? . . . A light what?

CORIE   Snow!

PAUL   (*Coming down the ladder*) Snow?? . . . It's going to snow tonight? . . . In here?

CORIE   They're wrong as often as they're right.

PAUL   I'm going to be shoveling snow in my own living room.

CORIE   It's a little hole.

PAUL   With that wind it could blow six-foot drifts in the bathroom. Honestly, Corie, I don't see how you can be so calm about all this.

CORIE   Well, what is it you want me to do?

PAUL   Go to pieces, like me. It's only natural.

CORIE   (*Goes to him and puts her arms around him*)   I've got a better idea. I'll keep you warm . . . And there's no charge for electricity . . .
    (*She kisses him*)

PAUL   I can see I haven't got much of a law career ahead of me.

CORIE   Good. I hope we starve. And they find us up here dead in each other's arms.

PAUL "Frozen skinny lovers found on Forty-eighth Street."
(*They kiss*)

CORIE   Are we in love again?

PAUL   We're in love again.
(*They kiss again, a long passionate embrace. The doorbell buzzes*)

CORIE (*Breaking away*)   The bed. I hope it's the bed. (*She buzzes back, and then opens the door and yells down*) Helllooooo! Bloomingdale's? (*From below, a female voice: Surprise!* CORIE *turns to* PAUL) Oh, God.

PAUL   What's wrong.

CORIE   Please, let it be a woman delivering the furniture.

PAUL   A woman?

VOICE   Corie?

CORIE   But it's my mother.

PAUL   Your mother? Now?

CORIE (*Taking off the nightgown and slipping into her top*)   She couldn't wait. Just one more day.

PAUL   Corie, you've got to get rid of her. I've got a case in court tomorrow.

CORIE   It's ugly in here without furniture, isn't it. She's just going to hate it, won't she?

VOICE Corie? Where are you?

CORIE (*Crosses to the door and yells down the stairs*) Up here, Mom. Top floor.

PAUL (*Hides the attaché case in a corner to the left of the windows*) How am I going to work tonight?

CORIE She'll think this is the way we're going to live. Like gypsies in an empty store. (*Attempting to button her top*)

PAUL (*Throwing the nightgown and lingerie into a suitcase*) Maybe I ought to sleep in the office.

CORIE She'll freeze to death. She'll sit there in her fur coat and freeze to death.

PAUL (*Helps her button her top*) I don't get you, Corie. Five minutes ago this was the Garden of Eden. Now it's suddenly Cannery Row.

CORIE She doesn't understand, Paul. She has a different set of values. She's practical. She's not young like us.

PAUL (*Gathers up the suitcase with lingerie and takes it into the bedroom*) Well, I'm twenty-six and cold as hell.

VOICE (*Getting nearer*) Corie?

CORIE (*Yells down at the door*) One more flight, Mother . . . Paul, promise me one thing. Don't tell her about the rent. If she asks, tell her you're not quite sure yet.

PAUL (*Crossing to the door with his coat collar up around his face*) Not sure what my rent is? I *have* to know what my rent is. I'm a college graduate.

CORIE (*Stopping* PAUL) Can't you lie a little? For me? You don't have to tell her it's a hundred and twenty-five.

PAUL All right. How much is it?

CORIE Sixty?

PAUL What?

CORIE Sixty-five?

PAUL Corie—

CORIE Seventy-five, all right? Seventy-five dollars and sixty-three cents a month. Including gas and electricity. She'll believe that, won't she?

PAUL *Anyone* would believe that. It's the hundred and twenty-five that's hard to swallow.
(*He combs his hair*)

CORIE She's taking a long time. I hope she's all right.

PAUL I can't lie about the stairs. She's going to figure out it's six floors all by herself.

CORIE Shh. Shh, she's here.
(*She starts to open the door*)

PAUL (*Grabs her*) Just promise *me* one thing. Don't let her stay too long because I've got a . . .

CORIE (*With him*) . . . case in court in the morning . . . I know, I know . . . (*She opens the door and goes into the hall*) . . . Mother!
> (MOTHER *shoots by her into the room and grabs the rail to keep from falling. She is in her late forties, pretty, but has not bothered to look after herself these past few years. She could use a permanent and a whole new wardrobe*)

PAUL (*Rushes to support her*) Hello, Mom.
> (MOTHER *struggles for air*)

MOTHER Oh! . . . Oh! . . . I can't breathe.

CORIE Take it easy, Mom.
> (*Holding her other arm*)

MOTHER I can't catch my breath.

PAUL You should have rested.

MOTHER I did . . . But there were always more stairs.

CORIE Paul, help her.

PAUL Come on, Mom. Watch the step.
> (*He starts to lead her up the step into the room*)

MOTHER More stairs?
> (*She steps up and* CORIE *and* PAUL *lead her toward* PAUL's *suitcase, still standing near the wall*)

CORIE You want some water?

MOTHER Later. I can't swallow yet.

PAUL Here, sit down.
   (*She sits on the suitcase*)

MOTHER Oh, my.

CORIE It's not *that* high, Mother.

MOTHER I know, dear. It's not bad really . . . What is it, nine flights?

PAUL Five. We don't count the stoop.

MOTHER I didn't think I'd make it . . . If I'd known the people on the third floor I'd have gone to visit them . . .
   (PAUL *sits on the bottom step of the ladder*)

CORIE This is a pleasant surprise, Mother.

MOTHER Well, I really had no intention of coming up, but I had a luncheon in Westchester and I thought, since it's on my way home, I might as well drop in for a few minutes . . .

CORIE On your way home to New Jersey?

MOTHER Yes. I just came over the Whitestone Bridge and down the Major Deegan highway and now I'll cut across town and onto the Henry Hudson Parkway and up to the George Washington Bridge. It's no extra trouble.

PAUL Sounds easy enough.

MOTHER Yes . . .

CORIE We were going to ask you over on Friday.

MOTHER Friday. Good. I'll be here Friday . . . I'm not going to stay now, I know you both must be busy.

PAUL Well, as a matter of fact . . .

CORIE (*Stopping him*) No, we're not, are we, Paul? (*He kills her with a glance*)

MOTHER Besides, Aunt Harriet is ringing the bell for me in ten minutes . . . Just one good look around, that's all. I'm not sure I'm coming back.

CORIE I wish you could have come an hour later. After the furniture arrived.

MOTHER (*Gets up, looks, and stops cold*) Don't worry. I've got a marvelous imagination.

CORIE Well . . . ?

MOTHER (*Stunned*) Oh, Corie . . . it's . . . beautiful.

CORIE You hate it . . .

MOTHER (*Moves toward windows*) No, no . . . It's a charming apartment. (*She trips over the platform*) I love it.

CORIE (*Rushes to her*) You can't really tell like this.

MOTHER I'm crazy about it.

CORIE It's not your kind of apartment. I knew you wouldn't like it.

MOTHER (*Moves down to* PAUL) I love it . . . Paul, didn't I say I loved it?
(*She takes his hand*)

PAUL She said she loved it.

MOTHER I knew I said it.

CORIE (*To* MOTHER) Do you really, Mother? I mean are you absolutely crazy in love with it?

MOTHER Oh, yes. It's very cute . . . And there's so much you can do with it.

CORIE I told you she hated it.

MOTHER (*Moves toward the bedroom landing*) Corie, you don't give a person a chance. At least let me see the whole apartment.

PAUL This *is* the whole apartment.

MOTHER (*Cheerfully*) It's a nice, large room.

CORIE There's a bedroom.

MOTHER Where?

PAUL One flight up.

CORIE It's four little steps. (*She goes up the steps to the bedroom door*) See. One-two-three-four.

MOTHER (*To* PAUL) Oh. Split-level. (*She climbs the steps*) And where's the bedroom? Through there?

CORIE No. *In* there. That's the bedroom . . . It's really just a dressing room but I'm going to use it as a bedroom.

MOTHER (*At the bedroom door*) That's a wonderful idea. And you can just put a bed in there.

CORIE That's right.

MOTHER How?
(PAUL *moves to the steps*)

CORIE It'll fit. I measured the room.

MOTHER A double bed?

CORIE No, an oversized single.

MOTHER Oh, they're nice. And where will Paul sleep?

CORIE With me.

PAUL (*Moves up on the landing*) In an oversized single?

MOTHER I'm sure you'll be comfortable.

CORIE I'm positive.
(PAUL *moves back down the stairs and glumly surveys the room*)

MOTHER It's a wonderful idea. Very clever . . .

CORIE Thank you.

MOTHER   Except you can't get to the closet.

CORIE   Yes you can.

MOTHER   Without climbing over the bed?

CORIE   No, you *have* to climb over the bed.

MOTHER   That's a good idea.

CORIE   (*Leaves the bedroom, crosses to the ladder, and climbs up*)   Everything's just temporary. As they say in *McCall's*, it won't really take shape until the bride's own personality becomes more clearly defined.

MOTHER   I think it's *you* right now. (*She turns to the other door*) What's in here? . . . (*She opens the door and looks in*) The bathroom . . . (*She closes the door*) No bathtub . . . You really have quite a lot here, for one room. (*She moves down the steps*) And where's the kitchen? (*She sees the stove and refrigerator, stops in horror, and then crosses toward the kitchen*) Whoo, there it is . . . Very cozy. I suppose you'll eat out a lot the first year.

CORIE   We're never eating out. It's big enough to make spaghetti and things.

MOTHER   What "things"?

CORIE   It's a dish I make called "Things." Honestly, Mother, we won't starve.

MOTHER   I know, dear. (*Under the skylight*) It's chilly in here. Do you feel a draft?

PAUL (*Looks up*) Uh, stand over here, Mom.
(*He moves her away from the hole to near the steam pipe next to the railing*)

CORIE What you need is a drink. Paul, why don't you run down and get some Scotch?

PAUL Now?

MOTHER (*Crossing toward the Franklin stove*) Oh, not for me. I'm leaving in a few minutes.

PAUL Oh. She's leaving in a few minutes.

CORIE She can stay for one drink.
(PAUL *quietly argues with* CORIE *at the ladder*)

MOTHER There's so much you can do in here. Lots of wall space. What color are you going to paint it?

CORIE It's painted.

MOTHER Very attractive.

PAUL (*Looks at his watch*) Wow. Nearly six.

MOTHER I've got to go.

CORIE Not until you have a drink . . . (*To* PAUL) Will you get the Scotch?
(*He continues to argue with her*)

MOTHER All right. I'll stay for just one drink.

33

PAUL   Good. I'll get the Scotch.
(*He starts for the door*)

MOTHER   Button up, dear. It's cold.

PAUL   I've noticed that.

CORIE   And get some cheese.
(PAUL *is gone*)

MOTHER   Paul! (PAUL *reappears at the door, and* MOTHER *extends her arms*) I just want to give my fella a kiss. And wish him luck. (PAUL *comes back in and crosses all the way over to* MOTHER. *She kisses him*) Your new home is absolutely beautiful. It's a perfect little apartment.

PAUL   Oh . . . thanks, Mom.

MOTHER   Then you *do* like it?

PAUL   Like it? (*He looks at* CORIE *and starts to exit*) Where else can you find anything like this . . . for seventy-five sixty-three a month?
(*He exits, leaving* CORIE *and* MOTHER *alone.* CORIE *climbs down the ladder, and looks for some sign of approval from* MOTHER)

CORIE   Well?

MOTHER   Oh, Corie, I'm so excited for you.
(*They embrace*)

CORIE   It's not exactly what you pictured, is it, Mother?

MOTHER   Well, it is *unusual*—like you. (*She crosses right*)

I remember when you were a little girl you said you wanted to live on the moon. (*She turns back to* CORIE) I thought you were joking . . . What about Paul? Is he happy with all this?

CORIE He's happy with me. I think it's the same thing. Why?

MOTHER I worry about you two. You're so impulsive. You jump into life. Paul is like me. He looks first. (*She sits down on the suitcase*)

CORIE He doesn't look. He stares. That's the trouble with both of you . . . (*She places a paint can next to* MOTHER *and sits on it*) Oh, Mother, you don't know how I dreaded your coming up here. I was sure you'd think I was completely out of my mind.

MOTHER Why should you think that, dear?

CORIE Well, it's the first thing I've ever done on my own. Without your help . . .

MOTHER If you wanted it, I'm sure you would have asked for it . . . but you didn't. And I understand.

CORIE I hope you do, Mother. It's something I just had to do all by myself.

MOTHER Corie, you mustn't think I'm hurt. I'm not hurt.

CORIE I'm so glad.

MOTHER You mustn't think I'm hurt. I don't get hurt over things like that.

CORIE I didn't think you would.

MOTHER *Other* things hurt me, but not that . . .

CORIE Good . . . Hey, let's open my presents and see what I've got. And you try to act surprised.
(*She gets the presents and brings them to the paint can*)

MOTHER You won't let me buy you anything . . . Oh, they're just a few little things.

CORIE (*Sitting down and shaking the smallest box vigorously*) What's in here? It sounds expensive.

MOTHER Well, *now* I think it's a broken clock.

CORIE (*Opens the box, and throws wrappings and tissue paper on the floor*) I'll bet you cleaned out Saks' gift department. I think I'm a regular stop on the delivery route now.
(*She looks at the clock, replaces it in the box and puts it aside, and begins to open the largest box*)

MOTHER Aunt Harriet was with me when I picked it out. (*She laughs*) She thinks I'm over here every day now.

CORIE You know you're welcome, Mother.

MOTHER I said, "Why, Harriet? Just because I'm alone now," I said. "I'm not afraid to live alone. In some ways it's better to live alone," I said. (CORIE *examines the blanket she finds in the package; then she closes the box, puts it aside, and begins to open the final package.*

MOTHER *picks up a piece of tissue paper and smoothes it out on her lap*) But, you can't tell her that. She thinks a woman living alone, way out in New Jersey, is the worst thing in the world . . . "It's not," I told her. "It's not the *worst* thing" . . .

CORIE (*She has opened the package and now takes out the dismantled parts of a coffee pot*) Hey, does this come with directions?

MOTHER If I knew about this kitchen, it would have come with hot coffee.
(*She laughs*)

CORIE (*Picks up the box with the clock and takes it with the parts of the coffee pot up into the kitchen*) Mother, you're an absolute angel. But you've got to stop buying things for me. It's getting embarrassing. (*She puts the clock on the refrigerator and the coffee pot on the sink*) If you keep it up I'm going to open a discount house . . .
(*She takes the blanket and places it with the suitcase near the windows*)

MOTHER It's my pleasure, Corie. (*She begins to gather up wrappings and tissue paper and place them in the box which contained the coffee pot*) It's a mother's greatest joy to be able to buy gifts for her daughter when she gets married. You'll see someday. I just hope your child doesn't deprive *you* of that pleasure.

CORIE I'm not depriving you, Mother.

MOTHER I didn't say you were.

CORIE (*Moves down to* MOTHER) Yes, you did.

MOTHER Then why are you?

CORIE Because I think you should spend the money on yourself, that's why.

MOTHER Myself? What does a woman like me need? Living all alone . . . Way out in New Jersey.
(*She picks up the box with wrappings in it and places it outside the front door*)

CORIE (*Follows* MOTHER) It's only been six days. And you're five minutes from the city.

MOTHER Who can get through that traffic in five minutes?

CORIE Then why don't you move into New York?

MOTHER Where . . . ? Where would I live?

CORIE Mother, I don't care where you live. The point is, you've got to start living for yourself now . . . (MOTHER *moves back into the room*) Mother, the whole world has just opened up to you. Why don't you travel? You've got the time, the luggage. All you need are the shots.

MOTHER (*Sits on the suitcase*) Travel! . . . You think it's so easy for a woman of my age to travel alone?

CORIE You'll meet people.

MOTHER I read a story in the *Times*. A middle-aged woman traveling alone fell off the deck of a ship. They never discovered it until they got to France.

CORIE (*Moves left and turns back to* MOTHER) I promise you, Mother, if *you* fell off a ship, *someone* would know about it.

MOTHER I thought I might get myself a job.

CORIE (*Straws in the wind*) Hey, that's a great idea.
(*She sits on the paint can*)

MOTHER (*Shrugs, defeated*) What would I do?

CORIE I don't know what you would do. What would you *like* to do?

MOTHER (*Considers*) I'd like to be a grandmother. I think that would be nice.

CORIE A grandmother??? . . . What's your rush? You know, underneath that Army uniform, you're still a young, vital woman . . . Do you know what I think you *really* need?

MOTHER Yes, and I don't want to hear it.
(*She gets up and moves away*)

CORIE (*Goes to her*) Because you're afraid to hear the truth.

MOTHER It's not the truth I'm afraid to hear. It's the *word* you're going to use.

CORIE You're darn right I'm going to use that word . . . It's love!

MOTHER Oh . . . Thank you.

39

CORIE   A week ago I didn't know what it meant. And then I checked into the Plaza Hotel. For six wonderful days . . . And do you know what happened to me there?

MOTHER   I promised myself I wouldn't ask.

CORIE   I found *love* . . . spiritual, emotional, and physical love. And I don't think anyone on earth should be without it.

MOTHER   I'm not. I have you.

CORIE   I don't mean *that* kind of love. (*She moves to the ladder and leans against it*) I'm talking about late at night in . . .

MOTHER (*Quickly*)   I *know* what you're talking about.

CORIE   Don't you even want to discuss it?

MOTHER   Not with *you* in the room.

CORIE   Well, what are you going to do about it?

MOTHER   I'm going back to New Jersey and give myself a Toni Home Permanent. Corie, sweetheart, I appreciate your concern, but I'm very happy the way I am.

CORIE   I'll be the judge of who's happy.
(*They embrace. The door flies open and* PAUL *staggers in with the bottle of Scotch. He closes the door behind him and wearily leans his head against it, utterly exhausted*)

MOTHER   Oh, Paul, you shouldn't have run . . . Just

for me. (*The doorbell buzzes,* AUNT HARRIET'S *special buzz*) . . . Ooh, and there's Harriet. I've got to go.
(*She picks up her purse from next to the suitcase*)

CORIE   Some visit.

MOTHER   Just a sneak preview. I'll see you on Friday for the World Première . . . (*To* PAUL) Good-bye, Paul . . . I'm so sorry . . . (*To* CORIE) Good-bye, love . . . I'll see you on Friday . . . (PAUL *opens the door for her*) Thank you . . . (*She glances out at the stairs*) Geronimo . . . !
(*She exits.* PAUL *shuts the door and, breathing hard, puts the bottle down at the foot of the ladder. He moves left, turns, and glares at* CORIE)

CORIE   What is it? . . . The stairs? (PAUL *shakes his head "No"*) The hole? (PAUL *shakes his head "No"*) The bathtub? (PAUL *shakes his head "No"*) Something new? (PAUL *nods his head "Yes"*) Well, what? . . .

PAUL (*Leaning against the left wall*)   Guess!

CORIE   Paul, I can't guess. Tell me.

PAUL   Oh, come on, Corie. Take a wild stab at it. Try something like, "All the neighbors are crazy."

CORIE   *Are* all the neighbors crazy?

PAUL (*A pitchman's revelation*)   I just had an interesting talk with the man down in the liquor store . . . Do you know we have some of the greatest weirdos in the country living right here, in this house?

41

CORIE Really? Like who?
(*She puts the bottle on the kitchen platform*)

PAUL (*Gathering his strength, he paces to the right*) Well, like to start with, in apartment One-C are the Boscos . . . Mr. and Mrs. J. Bosco.

CORIE (*Moving to the ladder*) Who are they?

PAUL (*Paces to the left*) Mr. and Mrs. J. Bosco are a lovely young couple who just happen to be of the same sex and no one knows which one that is . . . (*He moves up to left of the windows*) In apartment Three-C live Mr. and Mrs. Gonzales.

CORIE So?

PAUL (*Moves right above the ladder*) I'm not through. Mr. and Mrs. Gonzales, Mr. and Mrs. Armandariz, and Mr. Calhoun . . . (*He turns back to* CORIE) who must be the umpire. (*He moves left to left of the ladder, very secretively*) No one knows who lives in apartment Four-D. No one has come in or gone out in three years except every morning there are nine empty cans of tuna fish outside the door . . .

CORIE No kidding? Who do you think lives there?

PAUL Well, it sounds like a big cat with a can opener . . . (*He gets his attaché case from the corner, and turns to* CORIE) Now there *are* one or two normal couples in the building, but at this rent *we're* not one of them.

CORIE Well, you've got to pay for all this color and charm.

PAUL   Well, if you figure it that way, we're getting a bargain . . . (*He starts to go up the stairs, then turns back*) Oh, yes. I forgot. Mr. Velasco. Victor Velasco. He lives in apartment Six-A.

CORIE   Where's Six-A? (PAUL *points straight up*) On the roof?

PAUL   Attic . . . It's an attic. (*He crosses up onto the bedroom landing*) He also skis and climbs mountains. He's fifty-eight years old and he's known as "The Bluebeard of Forty-eighth Street."

CORIE (*Moves to the stairs*)   What does that mean?

PAUL (*Turns back to* CORIE)   Well, it either means that he's a practicing girl-attacker or else he's an old man with a blue beard. (*He moves to the bedroom*) I'll say this, Corie. It's not going to be a dull two years.

CORIE   Where are you going?

PAUL (*Turns back at the bedroom door*)   I'm going to stand in the bedroom and work. I've got to pay for all this color and charm. If anything comes up, like the furniture or the heat, let me know. Just let me know.
  (*Bows off into the bedroom and slams the door*)

CORIE (*After a moment of thought, she begins to fold up the ladder and put it against the left wall*)   Can't I come in and watch you? . . . Hey, Paul, I'm lonesome . . . (*There is a knock at the door*) . . . and scared! (*As* CORIE *puts the ladder against the wall,* VICTOR VELASCO, *fifty-eight and not breathing very hard, opens the door and enters. It's not that he is in such good shape. He just doesn't think about getting tired. There are too many other things to do in the world. He wears no topcoat. Just a sport jacket, an ascot, and a Tyrolean hat.* CORIE *turns and is startled to find him in the room)*

VELASCO I beg your pardon. *(He sweeps off his hat)* I hope I'm not disturbing you. I don't usually do this sort of thing but I find myself in a rather embarrassing position and I could use your help. *(He discreetly catches his breath)* My name is Velasco . . . Victor Velasco.

CORIE *(Nervously)* Oh, yes . . . You live in the attic.

VELASCO Yes. That's right . . . Have we met?

CORIE *(Very nervously)* No, not yet.

VELASCO Oh. Well, you see, I want to use your bedroom.

CORIE My bedroom?

VELASCO Yes. You see, I can't get into my apartment and I wanted to use your window. I'll just crawl out along the ledge.

CORIE Oh, did you lose your key?

VELASCO No. I have my key. I lost my money. I'm four months behind in the rent.

CORIE Oh! . . . Gee, that's too bad. I mean it's right in the middle of winter . . .

VELASCO You'll learn, as time goes by in this middle-

Robert Redford and Elizabeth Ashley as PAUL BRATTER and
CORIE BRATTER.

income prison camp, that we have a rat fink for a landlord . . . (*He looks about the room*) You don't have
any hot coffee, do you? I'd be glad to pay you for it.

CORIE No. We just moved in.

VELASCO Really? (*He looks about the barren room*)
What are you, a folksinger?

CORIE No. A wife . . . They didn't deliver our furniture
yet.

VELASCO (*Moves toward* CORIE) You know, of course,
that you're unbearably pretty. What's your name?

CORIE Corie . . . *Mrs.* Corie Bratter.

VELASCO (*Takes it in stride*) You're still unbearably
pretty. I may fall in love with you by seven o'clock.
(*Catching sight of the hole in the skylight*) I see the
rat fink left the hole in the skylight.

CORIE Yes, I just noticed that. (*She crosses right, and
looks up at the hole*) But he'll fix it, won't he?

VELASCO I wouldn't count on it. My bathtub's been running since 1949 . . . (*He moves toward* CORIE) Does
your husband work during the day?

CORIE Yes . . . Why? . . .

VELASCO It's just that I'm home during the day, and I
like to find out what my odds are . . . (*He scrutinizes*
CORIE) Am I making you nervous?

45

CORIE (*Moving away*) Very nervous.

VELASCO (*Highly pleased*) Good. Once a month, I try to make pretty young girls nervous just to keep my ego from going out. But, I'll save you a lot of anguish . . . I'm fifty-six years old and a thoroughly nice fellow.

CORIE Except I heard you were fifty-eight years old. And if you're knocking off two years, I'm nervous all over again.

VELASCO Not only pretty but bright. (*He sits down on the paint can*) I wish I were ten years older.

CORIE Older?

VELASCO Yes. Dirty old men seem to get away with a lot more. I'm still at the awkward stage . . . How long are you married?

CORIE Six days . . .

VELASCO In love? . . .

CORIE Very much . . .

VELASCO Damn . . .

CORIE What's wrong?

VELASCO Under my present state of financial duress, I was hoping to be invited down soon for a free meal. But, with newlyweds I could starve to death.

CORIE Oh. Well, we'd love to have you for dinner, as soon as we get set up.

VELASCO (*Gets up, and stepping over the suitcase, moves to* CORIE) I hate generalizations. When?

CORIE When? . . . Well, Friday? Is that all right?

VELASCO Perfect. I'll be famished. I hadn't planned on eating Thursday.

CORIE Oh, no . . . wait! On Friday night my mo— (*She thinks it over*) Yeah. Friday night will be fine.

VELASCO It's a date. I'll bring the wine. You can pay me for it when I get here . . . (*He moves to the stairs*) Which reminds me. You're invited to my cocktail party tonight. Ten o'clock . . . You do drink, don't you?

CORIE Yes, of course.

VELASCO Good. Bring liquor. (*He crosses to* CORIE *and takes her hand*) I'll see you tonight at ten.

CORIE (*Shivering*) If I don't freeze to death first.

VELASCO Oh, you don't know about the plumbing, do you? Everything in this museum works backward. (*Crosses to the radiator on the wall*) For instance, there's a little knob up there that says, "Important—Turn right" . . . So you turn left.
    (*He tries to reach it but can't*)

CORIE Oh, can you give me a little boost? . . .

VELASCO With the greatest of physical pleasure. One,

47

two, three . . . up . . . (*He puts his arms around her, and lifts her to the radiator*) Okay? . . .

CORIE (*Attempting to turn the knob*) I can't quite reach . . .

PAUL (*Comes out of the bedroom with an affidavit in his hand and his coat up over his head. He crosses to the head of the stairs*) Hey, Corie, when are they going to get here with—
(*He stops as he sees* CORIE *in* VELASCO's *arms.* VELASCO *looks at him, stunned, while* CORIE *remains motionless in the air*)

VELASCO (*Puts* CORIE *down*) I thought you said he works during the day.

CORIE Oh, Paul! This is Mr. Velasco. He was just showing me how to work the radiator.

VELASCO (*Extending his hand*) Victor Velasco! I'm your upstairs neighbor. I'm fifty-eight years old and a thoroughly nice fellow.

PAUL (*Lowers his coat, and shakes hands weakly*) Hello . . .

CORIE Mr. Velasco was just telling me that all the plumbing works backwards.

VELASCO That's right. An important thing to remember is, you have to flush "up." (*He demonstrates*) With that choice bit of information, I'll make my departure. (*He crosses up onto the bedroom landing*) Don't forget. Tonight at ten.

PAUL (*Looks at* CORIE) What's tonight at ten?

CORIE (*Moves to the bottom of the stairs*) Oh, thanks, but I don't think so. We're expecting our furniture any minute . . . Maybe some other time.

PAUL What's tonight at ten?

VELASCO I'll arrange it all for you in the morning. I'm also a brilliant decorator. (*He pats* PAUL *on the shoulder*) I insist you come.

CORIE Well, it's really very nice of you.

VELASCO (*Crossing to the bedroom door*) I told you. I'm a very nice person. *À ce soir* . . .
      (*He exits into the bedroom*)

PAUL (*To* CORIE) What's tonight at ten? . . . (*He suddenly realizes*) Where's he going? . . .
      (*He crosses to the bedroom*)

CORIE (*Yelling after* VELASCO) Don't forget Friday . . .

PAUL (*To* CORIE) What's he doing in the bedroom? . . . What about Friday?
      (*He goes into the bedroom*)

CORIE (*Rushes to the phone and dials*) He's coming to dinner. (*Into the phone*) Hello, Operator?

PAUL (*Comes out of the bedroom*) That nut went out the window.
      (*He looks back into the bedroom*)

CORIE I'm calling West Orange, New Jersey.

PAUL (*Crosses down the stairs to* CORIE) Corie, did you hear what I said? There's an old nut out on our ledge.

CORIE (*Into the phone*) Two, oh, one, seven, six, five, three, four, two, two.

PAUL Who are you calling?

CORIE My mother. On Friday night, she's going to have dinner with that old nut. (VELASCO *appears on the skylight, and carefully makes his way across.* CORIE *speaks into the phone*) Hello, Jessie . . . Will you please tell my mother to call me just as soon as she gets in!
(PAUL *turns and sees* VELASCO. VELASCO *cheerfully waves and continues on his way*)

Curtain

Act Two

ACT TWO

Scene One

Four days later. Seven o'clock, Friday evening.

The apartment is no longer an empty room. It is now a home. It is almost completely furnished, and the room, although a potpourri of various periods, styles, and prices, is extremely tasteful and comfortable. No ultramodern, clinical interior for CORIE. *Each piece was selected with loving care. Since* CORIE's *greatest aim in life is to spend as much time as possible alone with* PAUL, *she has designed the room to suit this purpose. A wrought-iron sofa stands in the middle of the room, upholstered in a bright striped fabric. It is flanked by two old-fashioned, unmatched armchairs, one with a romantically carved wooden back; the other, a bentwood chair with a black leather seat. A low, dark, wooden coffee table with carved legs is in front of the sofa, and to the right is a small, round bentwood end table, covered with green felt. Under the windows, a light-wood, Spanish-looking table serves as a desk, and in front of it is a bamboo, straight-backed chair. A large wicker basket functions as the wastebasket. A dark side table with lyre-shaped legs fills the wall under the radiator, and below the bedroom landing an open cane side table serves as a bar and telephone stand. To the right of the windows stands a breakfront with shelves above and drawers below. The kitchen area is now partially hidden by a four-fold bamboo screen that has been backed by fabric, and potted plants* have been placed in front of the screen. *Straight-backed bentwood chairs stand downstage right and left. The closet has been covered by a drapery, the small windows by café curtains, and the skylight by a large, striped Austrian curtain. Books now fill the bookcase left of the kitchen, pictures and decorations have been tastefully arranged on the walls, and lamps placed about the room. The bedroom landing is graced with a bentwood washstand complete with pitcher and basin which is filled with a plant. In the bathroom a shower curtain and towels have been hung, and the bedroom boasts a bed.*

AT RISE: *There is no one on stage. The apartment is dark except for a crack of light under the bedroom door, and faint moonlight from the skylight. Suddenly the front door opens and* CORIE *rushes in, carrying a pastry box and a bag containing two bottles. After switching on the lights at the door, she puts her packages on the coffee table, and hangs her coat in the closet.* CORIE *wears a cocktail dress for the festivities planned for tonight, and she sings as she hurries to get everything ready. She is breathing heavily but she is getting accustomed to the stairs. As she takes a bottle of vermouth and a bottle of gin out of the bag, the doorbell buzzes. She buzzes back, opens the door, and yells down the stairs.*

CORIE (*Yells*) Paul? (*We hear some strange, incoherent sound from below*) Hi, love . . . (*She crosses back to the coffee table, and dumps hors d'oeuvres from the pastry box onto a tray*) Hey, they sent the wrong lamps . . . but they go with the room so I'm keeping them. (*She crosses to the bar, gets a martini pitcher and brings it back to the coffee table*) . . . Oh, do you have an Aunt Fern? . . . Because she sent us a check . . . Anyway, you have a cheap Aunt Fern . . . How you doing? (*We hear a mumble from below.* CORIE *opens both bottles and pours them simultaneously into the shaker so that she has martinis made with equal parts of gin and vermouth)* . . . Oh, and your mother called from Philly . . . She and Dad will be up a week from Sunday . . . And your sister has a new boy friend. From Rutgers . . . He's got acne and they all hate him . . . including your sister. *(She takes the shaker and while mixing the cocktails she crosses to the door)* . . . Hey, lover, start puckering your lips 'cause you're gonna get kissed for five solid minutes and then . . . *(She stops)* Oh, hello, Mr. Munshin. I thought it was my husband. Sorry. *(A door slams. She shrugs sheepishly and walks back into the room, closing the door behind her. As she goes up into the kitchen, the door opens and* PAUL *enters, gasping. He drops his attaché case at the railing, and collapses on the couch.* CORIE *comes out of the kitchen with the shaker and ice bucket)* It was you. I thought I heard your voice.

(She puts the ice bucket on the bookcase and the shaker on the end table)

PAUL *(Gasp, gasp)* Mr. Munshin and I came in together. *(*CORIE *jumps on him and flings her arms around his neck; he winces in pain)* Do you have to carry on— a whole personal conversation with me—on the stairs?

CORIE Well, there's so much I wanted to tell you . . . and I haven't seen you all day . . . and it takes you so long to get up.

PAUL Everyone knows the intimate details of our life . . . I ring the bell and suddenly we're on the air.

CORIE Tomorrow I'll yell, "Come on up, Harry, my husband isn't home." (*She takes the empty box and bag, and throws them in the garbage pail in the kitchen*) Hey, wouldn't that be a gas if everyone in the building thought I was having an affair with someone?

PAUL Mr. Munshin thinks it's *him* right now.

CORIE (*Crossing back to the couch*) Well?

PAUL Well what?

CORIE What happened in court today? Gump or Birnbaum?

PAUL Birnbaum!

CORIE (*Jumps on his lap again. He winces again*) Oh, Paul, you won. You won, darling. Oh, sweetheart, I'm so proud of you. (*She stops and looks at him*) Well, aren't you happy?

PAUL (*Glumly*) Birnbaum won the protection of his good name but no damages. We were awarded six cents.

CORIE Six cents?

PAUL That's the law. You have to be awarded something, so the court made it six cents.

CORIE How much of that do you get?

PAUL Nothing. Birnbaum gets the whole six cents . . . And I get a going-over in the office. From now on I get all the cases that come in for a dime or under.

CORIE (*Opening his collar and rubbing his neck*) Oh, darling, you won. That's all that counts. You're a good lawyer.

PAUL Some lawyer . . . So tomorrow I go back to sharpening pencils.

CORIE And tonight you're here with me. (*She kisses his neck*) Did you miss me today?

PAUL No.

CORIE (*Gets off his lap and sits on the couch*) Why not?

PAUL Because you called me eight times . . . I don't speak to you that much when I'm home.

CORIE (*Rearranging the canapés*) Oh, you're grouchy. I want a divorce.

PAUL I'm not grouchy . . . I'm tired . . . I had a rotten day today . . . I'm a little irritable . . . and cold . . . and grouchy.

CORIE Okay, grouch. I'll fix you a drink. (*She crosses to the bar and brings back three glasses*)

PAUL (*Crosses to the closet, takes off his overcoat and jacket, and hangs them up*) I just couldn't think today. Couldn't think . . . Moving furniture until three o'clock in the morning.

CORIE Mr. Velasco moved. You complained.
(*She pours a drink*)

PAUL Mr. Velasco *pointed! I* moved! . . . He came in here, drank my liquor, made three telephone calls, and ordered me around like I was one of the Santini Brothers.
(He takes the drink from CORIE, *and crosses to the dictionary on the table under the radiator. He takes a gulp of his drink and reacts with horror. He looks at* CORIE, *who shrugs in reply)*

CORIE Temper, temper. We're supposed to be charming tonight.

PAUL *(Taking off his tie)* Yeah, well, I've got news for you. This thing tonight has "fiasco" written all over it.

CORIE *(Moves to the mirror on the washstand on the bedroom landing)* Why should it be a fiasco? It's just conceivable they may have something in common.

PAUL *(Folding his tie)* Your mother? That quiet, dainty little woman . . . and the Count of Monte Cristo? You must be kidding.
(He puts the tie between the pages of the dictionary, and slams it shut)

CORIE Why?
(She puts on a necklace and earrings)

PAUL *(Crosses to the closet and gets another tie)* You saw his apartment. He wears Japanese kimonos and sleeps on rugs. Your mother wears a hairnet and sleeps on a board.

CORIE What's that got to do with it?

PAUL (*Crossing back to the mirror under the radiator and fixing his tie*) Everything. He skis, climbs mountains, and the only way into his apartment is up a ladder or across a ledge. I don't really think he's looking for a good cook with a bad back.

CORIE The possibility of anything permanent never even occurred to me.

PAUL Permanent? We're lucky if we get past seven o'clock . . .
   (*The doorbell buzzes and* PAUL *crosses to the door*)

CORIE That's her. Now you've got me worried . . . Paul, did I do something horrible?

PAUL (*Buzzing downstairs*) Probably.

CORIE Well, do something. Don't answer the door. Maybe she'll go home.

PAUL Too late. I buzzed. I could put a few Nembutals in his drink. It won't stop him but it could slow him down. (*He opens the door and yells downstairs*) Mom?

MOTHER'S VOICE (*From far below*) Yes, dear . . .

PAUL (*Yelling through his hands*) Take your time. (*He turns back into the room*) She's at Camp Three. She'll try the final assault in a few minutes.

CORIE Paul, maybe we could help her.
   (*She comes down the stairs*)

59

PAUL (*Getting his blazer out of the closet*) What do you mean?

CORIE (*Behind the couch*) A woman puts on rouge and powder to make her face more attractive. Maybe we can put some make-up on her personality.

PAUL (*Puts his attaché case on the bookcase*) I don't think I want to hear the rest of this.

CORIE All I'm saying is, we don't have to come right out and introduce her as "my dull fifty-year-old housewife mother."

PAUL (*Crosses to the bar and pours a drink of Scotch*) Well, that wasn't the wording I had planned. What did you have in mind?

CORIE (*Moves around the couch and sits on the right side of the couch*) Something a little more glamorous . . . A former actress.

PAUL Corie—

CORIE Well, she *was* in *The Man Who Came to Dinner.*

PAUL Your mother? In *The Man Who Came to Dinner?* . . . Where, in the West Orange P.-T.A. show? (*He moves to the couch*)

CORIE No! . . . On Broadway . . . And she was in the original company of *Strange Interlude* and she had a small singing part in *Knickerbocker Holiday.*

PAUL Are you serious?

CORIE   Honestly. Cross my heart.

PAUL   Your mother? An actress?
(*He sits next to* CORIE)

CORIE   Yes.

PAUL   Why didn't you ever tell me?

CORIE   I didn't think you'd be interested.

PAUL   That's fascinating. I can't get over it.

CORIE   You see. *Now* you're interested in her.

PAUL   It's a lie?

CORIE   The whole thing.

PAUL   I'm going to control myself.
(*He gets up and crosses back of the couch*)

CORIE   (*Gets up and crosses to him at right of the couch*)
What do you say? Is she an actress?

PAUL   No.
(*He moves toward the door*)

CORIE   A fashion designer. The brains behind Ann Fogarty.

PAUL   (*Points to the door*)   She's on her way up.

CORIE   A mystery writer . . . under an assumed name.

PAUL   Let's lend her my trench coat and say she's a private eye.

CORIE   You're no help.

PAUL   I didn't book this act.

CORIE   (*Moves to* PAUL)   Paul, who is she going to be?

PAUL   She's going to be your mother . . . and the evening will eventually pass . . . It just means . . . that the Birdman of Forty-eighth Street, is not going to be your father. (*He opens the door*) Hello, Mom.
    (MOTHER *collapses in and* PAUL *and* CORIE *rush to support her. They quickly lead her to the armchair at right of the couch*)

CORIE   Hello, sweetheart, how are you? (*She kisses* MOTHER, *who gasps for air*) Are you all right? (MOTHER *nods*) You want some water?
    (MOTHER *shakes her head "No" as* PAUL *and* CORIE *lower her into the chair. She drops her pocketbook on the floor*)

MOTHER   Paul . . . in my pocketbook . . . are some pink pills.

PAUL   (*Picks up her bag, closes the door, and begins to look for the pills*) Pink pills . . .
    (CORIE *helps* MOTHER *take off her coat*)

MOTHER   I'll be all right . . . Just a little out of breath . . .
    (CORIE *crosses to the coffee table and pours a drink*)
I had to park the car six blocks away . . . then it started to rain so I ran the last two blocks . . . then my heel got

caught in the subway grating . . . so I pulled my foot out and stepped in a puddle . . . then a cab went by and splashed my stockings . . . if the hardware store downstairs was open . . . I was going to buy a knife and kill myself.

(PAUL *gives her a pill, and* CORIE *gives her a drink*)

CORIE   Here, Mom. Drink this down.

PAUL   Here's the pill . . .
(MOTHER *takes the pill, drinks, and coughs*)

MOTHER   A martini? To wash down a pill?

CORIE   It'll make you feel better.

MOTHER   I *had* a martini at home. It made me sick . . . That's why I'm taking the pill . . .
(CORIE *puts the drink down on the table*)

PAUL (*Sitting on the end table*)   You must be exhausted.

MOTHER   I'd just like to crawl into bed and cry myself to sleep.

CORIE (*Offering her the tray of hors d'oeuvres*)   Here, Mom, have an hors d'oeuvre.

MOTHER   No, thank you, dear.

CORIE   It's just blue cheese and sour cream.

MOTHER (*Holds her stomach*)   I wish you hadn't said that.

PAUL   She doesn't feel like it, Corie . . . (CORIE *puts the tray down and sits on the couch.* PAUL *turns to* MOTHER) Maybe you'd like to lie down?

CORIE (*Panicky*) Now? She can't lie down now.

MOTHER Corie's right. I can't lie down without my board . . . (*She puts her gloves into a pocket of her coat*) Right now all I want to do is see the apartment.

PAUL (*Sitting on the couch*) That's right. You haven't seen it with its clothes on, have you?

MOTHER (*Rises and moves to the left*) Oh, Corie . . . Corie . . .

CORIE She doesn't like it.

MOTHER (*Exhausted, she sinks into the armchair at left of the couch*) Like it? It's magnificent . . . and in less than a week. My goodness, how did you manage? Where did you get your ideas from?

PAUL We have a decorator who comes in through the window once a week.

CORIE (*Crossing to the bedroom*) Come take a look at the bedroom.

MOTHER (*Crossing to the bedroom*) Yes, that's what I want to do . . . look at the bedroom. Were you able to get the bed in? (*She looks into the room*) Oh, it just fits, doesn't it?

PAUL (*Moves to the stairs*) Just. We have to turn in unison.

MOTHER It looks very snug . . . and did you find a way to get to the closet?

CORIE Oh, we decided not to use the closet for a while.

MOTHER Really? Don't you need the space?

PAUL Not as much as we need the clothes. It flooded.

MOTHER The closet flooded?

CORIE It was an accident. Mr. Velasco left his bathtub running.

MOTHER (*Moving down the stairs*) Mr. Velasco . . . Oh, the man upstairs . . .

PAUL (*Taking her arm*) Oh, then you know about Mr. Velasco?

MOTHER Oh, yes. Corie had me on the phone for two hours.

PAUL Did you know he's been married three times?

MOTHER Yes . . . (*She turns back to* CORIE) If I were you, dear, I'd sleep with a gun. (*She sits in the bentwood armchair*)

PAUL Well, there's just one thing I want to say about this evening . . .

CORIE (*Quickly, as she crosses to the coffee table*) Er . . . not before you have a drink. (*She hands* MOTHER *the martini*) Come on, Mother. To toast our new home.

MOTHER (*Holding the glass*) Well, I can't refuse that.

CORIE (*Making a toast*) To the wonderful new life that's ahead of us all.

PAUL (*Holds up his glass*) And to the best sport I've ever seen. Your mother.

MOTHER (*Making a toast*) And to two very charming people . . . that I'm so glad to be seeing again tonight . . . your mother and father.
  (CORIE *sinks down on the sofa*)

PAUL (*About to drink, stops*) My what?

MOTHER Your mother and father.

PAUL What about my mother and father?

MOTHER Well, we're having dinner with them tonight, aren't we? . . . (*To* CORIE) Corie, isn't that what you said?

PAUL (*Sits next to* CORIE *on the sofa*) Is that right, Corie? Is that what you said?

CORIE (*Looks helpless, then plunges in*) Well, if I told you it was a blind date with Mr. Velasco upstairs, I couldn't have blasted you out of the house.

MOTHER A blind date . . . (*She doesn't quite get it yet*) With Mr. Velasco . . . (*Then the dawn*) The one that . . . ? (*She points up, then panics*) Good God!
  (*She takes a big gulp of her martini*)

PAUL (*To* CORIE) You didn't even tell your mother?

CORIE I was going to tell her the truth.

PAUL (*Looks at his watch*) It's one minute to seven. That's cutting it pretty thin, isn't it?

MOTHER Corie, how could you do this to me? Of all the people in the world . . .

CORIE (*Gets up and moves to* MOTHER) I don't see what you're making such a fuss about. He's just a man.

MOTHER My *accountant's* just a man. You make him sound like Douglas Fairbanks, Junior.

CORIE He looks *nothing* like Douglas Fairbanks, Junior, . . . does he, Paul?

PAUL No . . . He just jumps like him.

MOTHER I'm not even dressed.

CORIE (*Brushing her* MOTHER's *clothes*) You look fine, Mother.

MOTHER For Paul's parents I just wanted to look clean . . . *He'll* think I'm a nurse.

CORIE Look, Mother, I promise you you'll have a good time tonight. He's a sweet, charming, and intelligent man. If you'll just relax I *know* you'll have a perfectly nice evening. (*There is a knock on the door*) Besides, it's too late. He's here.

MOTHER Oh, no . . .

CORIE All right, now don't get excited.

MOTHER (*Gets up and puts her drink on the coffee table*)
You could say I'm the cleaning woman . . . I'll dust the
table. Give me five dollars and I'll leave.
 (*She starts up the stairs to the bedroom*)

CORIE (*Stops* MOTHER *on the stairs*) You just stay
here . . .

PAUL (*Going to* MOTHER) It's going to be fine, Mom.
 (*He crosses to the door*)

CORIE (*Leads* MOTHER *back to the sofa*) And smile.
You're irresistible when you do. And finish your martini.
 (*She takes it from the table and hands it to*
 MOTHER)

MOTHER Do you have a lot of these?

CORIE As many as you need.

MOTHER I'm going to need a lot of these.
 (*She downs a good belt*)

PAUL Can I open the door?

CORIE Paul, wait a minute . . . Mother . . . your hair
. . . in the back . . .

MOTHER (*Stricken, she begins to fuss with her hair*)
What? What's the matter with my hair?

CORIE (*Fixing* MOTHER's *hair*) It's all right now. I fixed it.

68

MOTHER (*Moves toward* PAUL) Is something wrong with my hair?

PAUL (*Impatient*) There's a man standing out there.

CORIE Wait a minute, Paul . . . (PAUL *moves back into the room and leans against the back of the armchair.* CORIE *turns* MOTHER *to her*) Now, Mother . . . The only thing I'd like to suggest is . . . well . . . just try and go along with everything.

MOTHER What do you mean? Where are we going?

CORIE I don't know. But wherever it is . . . just relax . . . and be one of the fellows.

MOTHER One of what fellows?

CORIE I mean, don't worry about your stomach. (*There is another knock on the door*)

MOTHER Oh, my stomach. (*She sinks down on the couch*)

PAUL Can I open the door now? . . .

CORIE (*Moving to the right of the couch*) Okay, okay . . . open the door. (PAUL *nods gratefully, then opens the door.* VE-LASCO *stands there, looking quite natty in a double-breasted, pin-striped blue suit. He carries a small covered frying pan in a gloved hand*)

PAUL Oh, sorry to keep you waiting, Mr. Velasco. Come on in . . .

VELASCO (*Moving into the well, to* PAUL) Ah! Ho si mah ling . . .

PAUL No, no . . . It's Paul.

VELASCO I know. I was just saying hello in Chinese . . .

PAUL Oh . . . hello.

VELASCO (*To* CORIE) Corie, rava-shing . . .

CORIE (*Enthralled*) Oh . . . What does that mean?

VELASCO Ravishing. That's English.

CORIE (*Taken aback*) Oh . . . Ah, Paul . . . Would you do the honors?

PAUL Yes, of course. Mr. Velasco, I'd like you to meet Corie's mother, Mrs. Banks . . . (CORIE *steps back, unveiling* MOTHER *with a gesture*) Mother, this is our new neighbor, Mr. Velasco . . .

MOTHER How do you do?

VELASCO (*Sweeps to* MOTHER, *takes her hand, and bows ever so slightly*) Mrs. Banks . . . I've been looking forward so to meeting you. I invite your daughter to my cocktail party and she spends the entire evening talking of nothing but you.
(CORIE *moves up to left of the couch, taking it all in with great pleasure*)

MOTHER Oh? . . . It must have been a dull party.

VELASCO   Not in the least.

MOTHER   I mean if she did nothing but talk about me
. . . *That* must have been dull. Not the party.
(PAUL *moves behind the couch to the coffee table
and gets his drink*)

VELASCO   I understand.

MOTHER   Thank you . . .

CORIE   (*To the rescue*)   Oh, is that for us?

VELASCO   Yes . . . I couldn't get the wine . . . my
credit stopped . . . so instead . . . (*He puts the pan
down on the end table and with a flourish lifts the cover*)
. . . Knichi!

MOTHER   Knichi?

CORIE   It's an hors d'oeuvre. Mr. Velasco makes them himself. He's a famous gourmet.

MOTHER   A gourmet . . . Imagine!

VELASCO   This won second prize last year at the Venice
Food Festival.

MOTHER   Second prize . . .

CORIE   Mr. Velasco once cooked for the King of Sweden,
Mother.

MOTHER   Really? Did you work for him?

VELASCO No . . . We belong to the same club.

MOTHER (*Embarrassed*) The same club . . . Of course.

VELASCO It's a Gourmet Society. There's a hundred and
fifty of us.

MOTHER All gourmets . . .

VELASCO That includes the King, Prince Phillip, and
Darryl Zanuck.

MOTHER Darryl Zanuck, too.

VELASCO We meet once every five years for a dinner that
we cook ourselves. In 1987 they're supposed to come to
my house. (*He looks at his watch*) We have another
thirty seconds . . .

PAUL Until what?

VELASCO Until they're edible. (*He takes the cover off the
pan, and puts it on the end table*) Now . . . the last
fifteen seconds we just let them sit there and breathe . . .

CORIE (*Moves to the right*) Gee, they look marvelous.

VELASCO When you eat this, you take a bite into history.
Knichi is over two thousand years old . . . Not this
particular batch, of course.
(*He laughs, but* MOTHER *laughs too loud and too
long*)

CORIE (*Again to the rescue*) Wow, what a great smell

. . . (*To* VELASCO) Mr. Velasco, would you be a traitor to the Society if you told us what's in it?

VELASCO (*Secretively*) Well, if caught, it's punishable by a cold salad at the dinner . . . but since I'm among friends, it's bits of salted fish, grated olives, spices, and onion biscuits . . . (MOTHER *reacts unhappily to the list of ingredients.* VELASCO *looks at his watch once more*) Ah, ready . . . Five, four, three, two, one . . . (*He holds the pan out to* MOTHER) Mrs. Banks?

MOTHER (*Tentatively*) Oh . . . thank you.
    (*She takes one and raises it slowly to her mouth*)

CORIE What kind of fish?

VELASCO Eel!

PAUL Eel?

MOTHER (*Crumples with distaste*) Eel??
    (*She doesn't eat it*)

VELASCO That's why the time element is so essential. Eel spoils quickly. (MOTHER *crumples even more*) Mrs. Banks, you're not eating.

MOTHER My throat's a little dry. Maybe if I finish my martini first . . .

VELASCO No, no . . . That will never do. The temperature of the knichi is very important. It must be now. In five minutes we throw it away.

MOTHER Oh! . . . Well, I wouldn't want you to do that.

73

(She looks at the knichi, then starts to take a nibble)

VELASCO Pop it!

MOTHER I beg your pardon?

VELASCO *(Puts down the pan and takes off his cooking glove)* If you nibble at knichi, it tastes bitter. You must pop it. *(He takes a knichi, tosses it from hand to hand three or four times and then pops it into his mouth)* You see.

MOTHER Oh, yes.
  (She tosses a knichi from hand to hand a few times and then tries to pop it into her mouth. But she misses and it flies over her shoulder. VELASCO quickly offers her another. Although this time she succeeds in getting it into her mouth, she chokes on it)

CORIE *(Sitting next to her)* Mother, are you all right?

MOTHER *(Coughing)* I think I popped it back too far.

CORIE *(Takes PAUL's drink from him and hands it to MOTHER)* Here . . . Drink this.

MOTHER *(Drinks, gasps)* Ooh . . . Was that my martini?

PAUL *(Gets up and retrieves his drink)* No. My Scotch.

MOTHER Oh, my stomach.

74

VELASCO (*Moving left behind the couch*) The trick is to pop it right to the center of the tongue . . . Then it gets the benefit of the entire palate . . . Corie?
(*He offers her the dish*)

CORIE (*Takes one*) Well, here goes. (*She tosses it back and forth, then pops it perfectly*) How about that?

VELASCO Perfect. You're the prettiest epicurean I've ever seen . . . (*He offers the knichi to* PAUL) Paul?

PAUL Er, no thank you. I have a bad arm.

CORIE You can *try* it. You should try everything, right, Mr. Velasco?

VELASCO As the French say, "At least once" . . . (PAUL *pulls up his sleeve, takes a knichi . . . then bites into it*) Agh . . . Bitter, right?

CORIE You know why, don't you?

PAUL I didn't pop! I nibbled!

CORIE Try another one and pop it.

PAUL I don't want to pop another one. Besides, I think we're over the five-minute limit now, anyway.

VELASCO (*Crossing to* MOTHER *behind the couch, he leans over to her very confidentially*) Taste is something that must be cultivated.

MOTHER (*Almost jumps*) Er, yes, I've often said that . . .

75

CORIE Well, are we ready to go out to dinner?

MOTHER (*Nervously*) You mean we're going out?

CORIE We had a fire in our stove.

MOTHER What happened?

PAUL Nothing. We just turned it on.

CORIE Mother, are you hungry?

MOTHER Not terribly . . . no.

CORIE Paul, you're the host. Suggest someplace.

PAUL Well . . . er . . . how about Marty's on Forty-seventh Street?

CORIE Marty's? That barn? You get a cow and a baked potato. What kind of a suggestion was that?

PAUL I'm sorry. I didn't know it was a trick question.

CORIE Tonight has to be something special. Mr. Velasco, you must know someplace different and unusual . . .

VELASCO (*Leaning against the end table*) Unusual? Yes, I know a very unusual place. It's the best food in New York. But I'm somewhat hesitant to suggest . . .

CORIE Oh, please. (*To* MOTHER) What do you say, Mother? Do you feel adventurous?

MOTHER You know me, one of the fellows.

CORIE (*To* VELASCO) There you are. We place the evening in your hands.

VELASCO A delightful proposition . . . For dinner, we go to the Four Winds.

PAUL Oh! The Chinese Restaurant? On Fifty-third Street?

VELASCO No . . . The Albanian restaurant on Staten Island.

MOTHER (*Holds her stomach*) Staten Island?

CORIE Doesn't it sound wild, Mother?

MOTHER Yes . . . wild.

CORIE I love it already.
(*As she sweeps past* PAUL *on her way to the bedroom, she punches him on the shoulder*)

VELASCO (*Sitting next to* MOTHER) Don't expect anything lavish in the way of decor. But Uzu will take care of the atmosphere.

MOTHER Who's Uzu?

VELASCO It's a Greek liqueur . . . Deceptively powerful. I'll only allow you one.

MOTHER Oh . . . thank you.

CORIE (*Coming out of the bedroom with her coat and purse*) It sounds perfect . . . Let's go.

PAUL It'll be murder getting a cab now.

VELASCO I'll worry about the transportation. All you have to do is pick up the check.

CORIE (*Back of the couch*) Mother has her car.

VELASCO (*Rises, and turns to* PAUL) You see? My job is done. Mrs. Banks . . .
(*He holds up her coat.* PAUL *crosses to the closet and gets his overcoat*)

MOTHER (*Putting on her coat*) Mr. Velasco, don't you wear a coat?

VELASCO Only in the winter.

MOTHER It's thirty-five.

VELASCO (*Taking a beret out of his pocket*) For twenty-five I wear a coat . . . For thirty-five . . . (*He puts the beret on, and crosses to the door taking a scarf out of his pocket with a great flair.* PAUL *watches with great distaste and then crosses into the bedroom and opens the door*) Ready? . . . My group stay close to me. If anyone gets lost, we'll meet at the United States Embassy.
(*He flings the scarf about his neck and exits.* MOTHER *desperately clutches* CORIE's *arm, but* CORIE *manages to push her out the door*)

CORIE (*Turning back for* PAUL) What are you looking for?

PAUL (*Comes out of the bedroom*) My gloves . . .

CORIE (*With disdain*) You don't need gloves. It's only thirty-five.

(*She sweeps out*)

PAUL That's right. I forgot. (*Mimicking* VELASCO, *he flings his scarf around his neck as he crosses to the door*) We're having a heat wave. (*He turns off the lights and slams the door shut*)

Curtain

(*In the dark we hear the splash of waves and the melancholy toots of foghorns in the harbor sounding almost as sad as* PAUL *and* MOTHER *must be feeling at this moment*)

Scene Two

About 2:00 A.M.

The apartment is still dark. We hear laughter on the stairs. The door opens and CORIE *rushes in. She is breathless, hysterical, and wearing* VELASCO's *beret and scarf.*

CORIE Whoo . . . I beat you . . . I won.
(*She turns on the lights, crosses to the couch, and collapses on it.* VELASCO *rushes in after her, breathless and laughing*)

VELASCO (*Sinking to the floor in front of the couch*) It wasn't a fair race. You tickled me.

CORIE Ooh . . . Ooh, I feel good. Except my tongue keeps rolling up. And when I talk it rolls back out like a noisemaker.

VELASCO That's a good sign. It shows the food was seasoned properly.

CORIE Hey, tell me how to say it again.

VELASCO Say what?

CORIE "Waiter, there's a fly in my soup."

VELASCO Oh. "Poopla . . . sirca al mercoori."

CORIE That's right. "Sirca . . . poopla al mercoori."

VELASCO No, no. That's "Fly, I have a waiter in my soup."

CORIE Well, I did. He put in his hand to take out the fly. (*She rises to her knees*) Boy, I like that singer . . . (*She sways back and forth as she sings*) "Shama . . . shama . . . ela mal kemama" . . . (*She flings her coat onto the couch.* VELASCO *rises to a sitting position, crosses his legs, and plays an imaginary flute*) Hey, what am I singing, anyway?

VELASCO (*Stretches prone on the floor*) It's an old Albanian folk song.

CORIE (*Impressed with her own virtuosity*) "Shama shama . . ."? No kidding? What does it mean?

VELASCO "Jimmy cracked corn and I don't care."

CORIE Well, I don't. (*She feels her head*) Oh, boy . . . How many Zuzus did I have? Three or four?

VELASCO *U*zus! . . . Nine or ten.

CORIE Then it was ten 'cause I thought I had four . . . How is my head going to feel in the morning?

VELASCO Wonderful.

CORIE No headaches?

VELASCO No headache . . . But you won't be able to make a fist for three days.

(*He raises his hands and demonstrates by not being able to make a fist*)

CORIE (*Holds out both hands and looks at them*)   Yeah. Look at that. Stiff as a board. (*She climbs off the couch, and moves onto the floor next to* VELASCO) What do they put in Uzu anyway?

VELASCO (*Holding up stiff hands*)   I think it's starch.

CORIE (*Looks at her two stiff hands*)   . . . Hey, how about a game of ping-pong? We can play doubles.
(CORIE *swings her two stiff hands at an imaginary ball*)

VELASCO   Not now. (*He sits up*) We're supposed to do something important. What was it?

CORIE   What was it? (*She ponders, then remembers*) Oh! . . . We're supposed to make coffee.
(CORIE *places the shoes she has taken off under the sofa and moves toward the kitchen*)

VELASCO (*Following her*)   I'll make it. What kind do you have?

CORIE   Instant Maxwell House.

VELASCO (*Crushed*)   *Instant* coffee?
(*He holds his brow with his stiff hands. He and* CORIE *disappear behind the screened kitchen continuing their babbling. Suddenly we hear scuffling in the hallway and* PAUL *struggles in through the door carrying* MOTHER *in his arms. From* PAUL's *staggering we'd guess that* MOTHER *must now weigh*

about two thousand pounds. He makes it to the sofa, where he drops her, and then sinks in utter exhaustion to the floor below her. They both stare unseeing, and suck desperately for air. CORIE *and* VELASCO, *who carries a coffee pot, emerge from the kitchen)*

CORIE *(Crosses to* MOTHER*)* Forgot the stove doesn't work. Upstairs, everyone . . . for coffee. *(*CORIE *pulls* MOTHER'*s coat but there is no reaction from* MOTHER *or* PAUL*)* Don't you want coffee?
*(*PAUL *and* MOTHER *shake their heads "No")*

VELASCO *(Going to the door)* They'll drink it if we make it . . .

CORIE *(Following him)* Don't you two go away . . .
*(*CORIE *and* VELASCO *exit, both singing "Shama, shama."* PAUL *and* MOTHER *stare silently ahead. They appear to be in shock, as if having gone through some terrible ordeal)*

MOTHER *(Finally)* . . . I feel like we've died . . . and gone to heaven . . . only we had to climb up . . .

PAUL *(Gathering his strength)* . . . Struck down in the prime of life . . .

MOTHER . . . I don't really feel sick . . . Just kind of numb . . . and I can't make a fist . . .
(She holds up a stiff hand)

PAUL You want to hear something frightening? . . . My teeth feel soft . . . It's funny . . . but the best thing we had all night was the knichi.

MOTHER Anyway, Corie had a good time . . . Don't you think Corie had a good time, Paul?

PAUL (*Struggling up onto the couch*) Wonderful . . . Poor kid . . . It isn't often we get out to Staten Island in February.

MOTHER She seems to get such a terrific kick out of living. You've got to admire that, don't you, Paul?

PAUL I admire anyone who has three portions of pooflapoo pie.

MOTHER (*Starts*) What's poofla-poo pie?

PAUL Don't you remember? That gook that came in a turban.

MOTHER I thought that was the waiter . . . I tried, Paul. But I just couldn't seem to work up an appetite the way they did.

PAUL (*Reassuring her*) No, no, Mom . . . You mustn't blame yourself . . . We're just not used to that kind of food . . . You just don't pick up your fork and dig into a *brown* salad . . . You've got to play around with it for a while.

MOTHER Maybe I *am* getting old . . . I don't mind telling you it's very discouraging . . . (*With great difficulty, she manages to rouse herself and get up from the couch*) Anyway, I don't think I could get through coffee . . . I'm all out of pink pills . . .

PAUL Where are you going?

MOTHER Home . . . I want to die in my own bed. (*Exhausted, she sinks into a chair*)

PAUL Well, what'll I tell them?

MOTHER Oh, make up some clever little lie. (*She rallies herself and gets up*) Tell Corie I'm not really her mother. She'll probably never want to see me again anyway . . . Good night, dear. (*Just as* MOTHER *gets to the door, it opens and* CORIE *and* VELASCO *return*) Oh, coffee ready? (*She turns back into the room.* VELASCO *crosses to the bar as* CORIE *moves to behind the couch*)

CORIE I was whistling the Armenian National Anthem and I blew out the pilot light.

VELASCO (*Puts four brandy snifters he has brought in down on the bar, and taking a decanter from the bar begins to pour brandy*) Instead we're going to have flaming brandy . . . Corie, give everyone a match.
(CORIE *moves to the side table*)

MOTHER I'm afraid you'll have to excuse me, dear. It *is* a little late.

CORIE (*Moves toward* MOTHER) Mother, you're not going home. It's the shank of the evening.

MOTHER I know, but I've got a ten-o'clock dentist appointment . . . at nine o'clock . . . and it's been a very long evening . . . What I mean is it's late, but I've had a wonderful time . . . I don't know what I'm saying.

CORIE But, Mother . . .

MOTHER Darling, I'll call you in the morning. Good night, Paul . . . Good night, Mr. Velasco . . .

VELASCO (*Putting down the brandy, he crosses to* CORIE) Good night, Paul . . . Good night, Corie . . .

CORIE Mr. Velasco, you're not going, too?

VELASCO (*Taking his beret and scarf from* CORIE *and putting them on*) Of course. I'm driving Mrs. Banks home.

MOTHER (*Moves away in shock*) Oh, no! . . . (*She recovers herself and turns back*) I mean, oh, no, it's too late.

VELASCO (*To* MOTHER) Too late for what?

MOTHER The buses. They stop running at two. How will you get home?

VELASCO Why worry about it now? I'll meet that problem in New Jersey.
  (VELASCO *moves to the door and* CORIE *in great jubilation flings herself over the back of the couch*)

MOTHER And it's such a long trip . . . (*She crosses to* CORIE) Corie, isn't it a long trip?

CORIE Not really. It's only about thirty minutes.

MOTHER But it's such an inconvenience. Really, Mr. Velasco, it's very sweet of you but—

VELASCO Victor!

86

MOTHER What?

VELASCO If we're going to spend the rest of the evening together, it must be Victor.

MOTHER Oh!

VELASCO And I insist the arrangement be reciprocal. What is it?

MOTHER What is what?

CORIE Your name, Mother. (*To* VELASCO) It's Ethel.

MOTHER Oh, that's right. Ethel. My name is Ethel.

VELASCO That's better . . . Now . . . are we ready . . . Ethel?

MOTHER Well . . . if you insist, Walter.

VELASCO Victor! It's Victor.

MOTHER Yes. Victor!

VELASCO Good night, Paul . . . Shama shama, Corie.

CORIE Shama shama!

VELASCO (*Moves to the door*) If you don't hear from us in a week, we'll be at the Naciónal Hotel in Mexico City . . . Room seven-oh-three! . . . Let's go, Ethel!
    (*And he goes out the door.* MOTHER *turns to* CORIE *and looks for help*)

87

MOTHER (*Frightened, she grabs* CORIE's *arm*) What does he mean by that?

CORIE I don't know, but I'm dying to find out. Will you call me in the morning?

MOTHER Yes . . . about six o'clock!
(*And in a panic, she exits*)

CORIE (*Takes a beat, closes the door, smiles, and turns to* PAUL) Well . . . how about *that*, Mr. "This is going to be a fiasco tonight"? . . . He's taking her all the way out to New Jersey . . . at two o'clock in the morning . . . That's what I call "The Complete Gentleman" . . . (PAUL *looks at her with disdain, rises and staggers up the stairs into the bedroom*) He hasn't even given a thought about how he's going to get home . . . Maybe he'll sleep over . . . Hey, Paul, do you think . . . ? No, not my mother . . . (*She jumps up onto the couch*) Then again anything can happen with Rupert of Henzau . . . Boy, what a night . . . Hey! I got a plan. Let's take the bottle of Scotch downstairs, ring all the bells and yell "Police" . . . Just to see who comes out of whose apartment . . . (*There is no answer from the bedroom*) . . . Paul? . . . What's the matter, darling? . . . Don't you feel well?

PAUL (*Comes out of the bedroom, down the stairs, and crosses to the closet. He is taking his coat off and is angry*) What a rotten thing to do . . . To your own mother.

CORIE What?

PAUL   Do you have any idea how she felt just now? Do
you know what kind of a night this was for her?

CORIE (*Impishly*)   It's not over yet.

PAUL   You didn't see her sitting here two minutes ago.
You were upstairs with that Hungarian Duncan Hines
. . . Well, she was miserable. Her face was longer than
that trip we took tonight.
(*He hangs up his coat in the closet*)

CORIE   She never said a thing to me.

PAUL (*Takes out a hanger and puts his jacket on it*)   She's
too good a sport. She went the whole cockeyed way . . .
Boy, oh boy . . . dragging a woman like that all the way
out to the middle of the harbor for a bowl of sheep dip.
(*He hangs his jacket up and crosses to the dictionary on the side table under the radiator. He takes
his tie off and folds it neatly*)

CORIE (*Follows him to the table*)   It was Greek bean soup.
And at least *she* tasted it. She didn't jab at it with her
knife, throwing cute little epigrams like, "Ho, ho, ho
. . . I think there's someone in there."

PAUL (*Puts the tie between pages of the dictionary*)
That's right. That's right. At least I was honest about it.
You ate two bowls because you were showing off for Al
Capone at the next table.
(PAUL *searches for his wallet unsuccessfully*)

CORIE   What are you so angry about, Paul?

PAUL (*Crossing to the closet*) I just told you. I felt terrible for your mother.
(*He gets the wallet out of his jacket pocket*)

CORIE (*Following after him to the front of the couch*) Why? Where is she at this very minute? Alone with probably the most attractive man she's ever met. Don't tell me *that* doesn't beat hell out of hair curlers and the "Late Late Show."

PAUL (*Crossing onto bedroom landing*) Oh, I can just hear it now. What sparkling conversation. He's probably telling her about a chicken cacciatore he once cooked for the High Lama of Tibet and she's sitting there shoving pink pills in her mouth.

CORIE (*Taking her coat from the couch and putting it on the armchair at right*) You never can tell what people talk about when they're alone.

PAUL I don't understand how you can be so unconcerned about this.
(*He goes into the bedroom*)

CORIE (*Moving to the stairs*) Unconcerned . . . I'm plenty concerned. Do you think I'm going to get one wink of sleep until that phone rings tomorrow? I'm scared to death for my mother. But I'm grateful there's finally the opportunity for something to be scared about . . . (*She moves right, then turns back*) What I'm really concerned about is *you*!

PAUL (*Bursts out of the bedroom, nearly slamming through the door*) Me? Me?

CORIE I'm beginning to wonder if you're capable of *having* a good time.

PAUL Why? Because I like to wear my gloves in the winter?

CORIE No. Because there isn't the least bit of adventure in you. Do you know what you are? You're a Watcher. There are Watchers in this world and there are Do-ers. And the Watchers sit around watching the Do-ers do. Well, tonight you watched and I did.

PAUL (*Moves down the stairs to* CORIE) Yeah . . . Well, it was harder to watch what you did than it was for you to *do* what I was watching.
    (*He goes back up the stairs to the landing*)

CORIE You won't let your hair down for a minute? You couldn't even relax for one night. Boy, Paul, sometimes you act like a . . . a . . .
    (*She gets her shoes from under the couch*)

PAUL (*Stopping on the landing*) What . . . ? A stuffed shirt?

CORIE (*Drops the shoes on the couch*) I didn't say that.

PAUL That's what you're implying.

CORIE (*Moves to the right armchair and begins to take off her jewelry*) That's what you're anticipating. I didn't say you're a stuffed shirt. But you are extremely proper and dignified.

PAUL I'm proper and dignified? (*He moves to* CORIE) When . . . ? When was I proper and dignified?

CORIE (*Turns to* PAUL) All right. The other night. At Delfino's . . . You were drunk, right?

PAUL Right. I was stoned.

CORIE There you are. I didn't know it until you told me in the morning. (*She unzips her dress and takes it off*) You're a funny kind of drunk. You just sat there looking unhappy and watching your coat.

PAUL I was watching my coat because I saw someone else watching my coat . . . Look, if you want, I'll get drunk for you sometime. I'll show you a slob, make your hair stand on end.
(*He unbuttons his shirt*)

CORIE (*Puts her dress on the chair*) It isn't necessary.

PAUL (*Starts to go, turns back*) Do you know . . . Do you know, in P. J. Clarke's last New Year's Eve, I punched an old woman . . . Don't tell me about drunks.
(*He starts to go*)

CORIE (*Taking down her hair*) All right, Paul.

PAUL (*Turns back and moves to behind the couch*) When else? When else was I proper and dignified?

CORIE Always. You're always dressed right, you always look right, you always say the right things. You're very close to being perfect.

Mildred Natwick, Elizabeth Ashley, Kurt Kazner, and Robert Redford, as MRS. BANKS, CORIE BRATTER, VICTOR VELASCO, and PAUL BRATTER.

PAUL (*Hurt to the quick*) That's . . . that's a *rotten* thing to say.

CORIE (*Moves to* PAUL) I have never seen you without a jacket. I always feel like such a slob compared to you. Before we were married I was sure you slept with a tie.

PAUL No, no. Just for very *formal* sleeps.

CORIE You can't even walk into a candy store and ask the lady for a Tootsie Roll. (*Playing the scene out, she moves down to right side of the couch*) You've got to walk up to the counter and point at it and say, "I'll have that thing in the brown and white wrapper."

PAUL (*Moving to the bedroom door*) That's ridiculous.

CORIE And you're not. That's just the trouble. (*She crosses to the foot of the stairs*) Like Thursday night. You wouldn't walk barefoot with me in Washington Square Park. Why not?

PAUL (*Moving to the head of the stairs*) Very simple answer. It was seventeen degrees.

CORIE (*Moves back to the chair and continues taking down her hair*) Exactly. That's very sensible and logical. Except it isn't any fun.

PAUL (*Moves down the stairs to the couch*) You know maybe I *am* too proper and dignified for you. Maybe you would have been happier with someone a little more colorful and flamboyant . . . like the Geek!
(*He starts back to the bedroom*)

CORIE Well, he'd be a lot more laughs than a stuffed shirt.

PAUL (*Turns back on the landing*) Oh, oh . . . I thought you said I wasn't.

CORIE Well, you are now.

PAUL (*Reflectively*) I'm not going to listen to this . . . I'm not going to listen . . . (*He starts for the bedroom*) I've got a case in court in the morning.

CORIE (*Moves left*) Where are you going?

PAUL To sleep.

CORIE Now? How can you sleep now?

PAUL (*Steps up on the bed and turns back, leaning on the door jamb*) I'm going to close my eyes and count knichis. Good night!

CORIE You can't go to sleep now. We're having a fight.

PAUL *You* have the fight. When you're through, turn off the lights.
(*He turns back into the bedroom*)

CORIE Ooh, that gets me insane. You can even control your emotions.

PAUL (*Storms out to the head of the stairs*) Look, I'm just as upset as you are . . . (*He controls himself*) But when I get hungry, I eat. And when I get tired, I sleep. You eat and sleep, too. Don't deny it, I've seen you . . .

CORIE (*Moves right with a grand gesture*) Not in the middle of a crisis.

PAUL What crisis? We're just yelling a little.

CORIE You don't consider this a crisis? Our whole marriage hangs in the balance.

PAUL (*Sits on the steps*) It does? When did that happen?

CORIE Just now. It's suddenly very clear that you and I have absolutely *nothing* in common.

PAUL Why? Because I won't walk barefoot in the park in winter? You haven't got a case, Corie. Adultery, yes. Cold feet, no.

CORIE (*Seething*) Don't oversimplify this. I'm angry. Can't you see that?

PAUL (*Brings his hands to his eyes, peers at her through imaginary binoculars, and then looks at his watch*) Corie, it's two-fifteen. If I can fall asleep in about half an hour, I can get about five hours' sleep. I'll call you from court tomorrow and we can fight over the phone. (*He gets up and moves to the bedroom*)

CORIE You will *not* go to sleep. You will stay here and fight to save our marriage.

PAUL (*In the doorway*) If our marriage hinges on breathing fish balls and poofla-poo pie, it's not worth saving . . . I am now going to crawl into our tiny, little, single bed. If you care to join me, we will be sleeping from left to right tonight.

95

(He goes into the bedroom and slams the door)

CORIE   You won't discuss it . . . You're *afraid* to discuss it . . . I married a coward!! . . .
(She takes a shoe from the couch and throws it at the bedroom door)

PAUL   *(Opens the door)*   Corie, would you bring in a pail? The closet's dripping.

CORIE   Ohh, I hate you! I hate you! I really, really hate you!

PAUL   *(Storms to the head of the stairs)*   Corie, there is one thing I learned in court. Be careful when you're tired and angry. You might say something you will soon regret. I-am-now-tired-and-angry.

CORIE   And a coward.

PAUL   *(Comes down the stairs to her at right of the couch)*   And I will now say something I will soon regret . . . Okay, Corie, maybe you're right. Maybe we have nothing in common. Maybe we rushed into this marriage a little too fast. Maybe Love isn't enough. Maybe two people should have to take more than a blood test. Maybe they should be checked for common sense, understanding, and emotional maturity.

CORIE   *(That hurt)*   All right . . . Why don't you get it passed in the Supreme Court? Only those couples bearing a letter from their psychiatrists proving they're well-adjusted will be permitted to be married.

PAUL   You're impossible.

CORIE   You're unbearable.

PAUL   You belong in a nursery school.

CORIE   It's a lot more fun than the Home for the Fuddy Duddies.

PAUL   (*Reaches out his hand to her*)   All right, Corie, let's not get . . .

CORIE   Don't you touch me . . . Don't you touch me . . . (PAUL *very deliberately reaches out and touches her.* CORIE *screams hysterically and runs across the room, away from him. Hysterically*) I don't want you near me. Ever again.

PAUL   (*Moves toward her*)   Now wait a minute, Corie—

CORIE   No. (*She turns away from him*) I can't look at you. I can't even be in the same room with you now.

PAUL   Why?

CORIE   I just can't, that's all. Not when you feel this way.

PAUL   When I feel what way?

CORIE   The way you feel about me.

PAUL   Corie, you're hysterical.

CORIE   (*Even more hysterically*)   I am not hysterical. I know exactly what I'm saying. It's no good between us, Paul. It never will be again.

PAUL (*Throwing up his hands and sinking to the couch*)
Holy cow.

CORIE   I'm sorry, I— (*She fights back tears*) I don't want
to cry.

PAUL   Oh, for pete's sakes, cry. Go ahead and cry.

CORIE (*At the height of fury*)   Don't you tell me when to
cry. I'll cry when I want to cry. And I'm not going to
have my cry until you're out of this apartment.

PAUL   What do you mean, "out of this apartment"?

CORIE   Well, you certainly don't think we're going to
live here together, do you? After tonight?

PAUL   Are you serious?

CORIE   Of course I'm serious. *I want a divorce!*

PAUL (*Shocked, he jumps up*)   A *divorce?* What?

CORIE (*Pulls herself together, and with great calm, begins
to go up the stairs*)   I'm sorry, Paul, I can't discuss it
any more. Good night.

PAUL   Where are you going?

CORIE   To bed.
(*She turns back to* PAUL)

PAUL   You can't. Not now.

CORIE   You did before.

PAUL   That was in the middle of a fight. This is in the middle of a divorce.

CORIE   I can't talk to you when you're hysterical. Good night.
(She goes into the bedroom)

PAUL   Will you come here? . . . (CORIE *comes out on the landing*) I want to know why you want a divorce.

CORIE   I told you why. Because you and I have absolutely nothing in common.

PAUL   What about those six days at the Plaza?

CORIE   (*Sagely*) Six days does not a week make.

PAUL   (*Taken aback*) What does *that* mean?

CORIE   I don't know what it means. I just want a divorce.

PAUL   You know, I think you really mean it.

CORIE   I *do!*

PAUL   You mean, every time we have a little fight, you're going to want a divorce?

CORIE   (*Reassuring*) There isn't going to be any more little fights. This is it, Paul! This is the end. Good night.
(She goes into the bedroom and closes the door behind her)

PAUL   Corie, do you mean to say— (*He yells*) Will you come down here?!

CORIE (*Yells from the bedroom*) Why?

PAUL (*Screams back*) Because I don't want to yell. (*The door opens and* CORIE *comes out. She stands at the top of the stairs. He points to his feet*) All the way.

CORIE (*Seething, comes all the way down and stands where he pointed*) Afraid the crazy neighbors will hear us?

PAUL You're serious.

CORIE Dead serious.

PAUL You mean the whole thing? With signing papers and going to court, shaking hands, good-bye, finished, forever, divorced?

CORIE (*Nodding in agreement*) That's what I mean . . .

PAUL I see . . . Well . . . I guess there's nothing left to be said.

CORIE I guess not.

PAUL Right . . . Well, er . . . Good night, Corie. (*And he goes up the stairs*)

CORIE Where are you going?

PAUL (*Turns back on the landing*) To bed.

CORIE Don't you want to talk about it?

PAUL At two-thirty in the morning?

CORIE I can't sleep until this thing is settled.
(*She moves to the couch*)

PAUL Well, it may take three months. Why don't you at least take a *nap?*

CORIE You don't have to get snippy.

PAUL Well, dammit, I'm sorry, but when I plan vacations I'm happy and when I plan divorces I'm snippy. (*He crosses to the bookcase and grabs his attaché case*) All right, you want to plan this thing, let's plan it. (*He storms to the coffee table and sweeps everything there onto the floor with his hand*) You want a quick divorce or a slow painful one?

CORIE (*Horrified*) I'm going to bed.
(*She goes up the stairs*)

PAUL (*Shouts*) You stay here or you get no divorce from me.

CORIE (*Stops on the landing*) You can try acting civilized.

PAUL (*Putting down the attaché case*) Okay, I'll be civilized. But charm you're not going to get. (*He pushes a chair toward her*) Now sit down! . . . Because there's a lot of legal and technical details to go through.
(*He opens the attaché case*)

CORIE Can't you do all that? I don't know anything about legal things.

PAUL (*Wheels on her and in a great gesture points an accusing finger at her*) Ah, haa . . . Now *I'm* the Do-er and *you're* the Watcher! (*Relentlessly*) Right, Corie? Heh? Right? Right? Isn't that right, Corie?

CORIE (*With utmost disdain*) . . . So this is what you're *really* like!

PAUL (*Grimacing like the monster he is*) Yes . . . Yes . . .

CORIE (*Determined she's doing the right thing. She comes down the stairs, and sits, first carefully moving the chair away from* PAUL) All right, what do I have to do?

PAUL First of all, what grounds?
(*He sits on the couch*)

CORIE (*Not looking at* PAUL) Grounds?

PAUL (*Taking a legal pad and a pencil out of the case*) That's right. Grounds. What is your reason for divorcing me? And remember, my failure to appreciate knichis will only hold up in a Russian court.

CORIE You're a scream, Paul. Why weren't you funny when we were happy?

PAUL Okay . . . How about incompatible?

CORIE Fine. Are you through with me?

PAUL Not yet. What about the financial settlement?

CORIE I don't want a thing.

PAUL Oh, but you're entitled to it. Alimony, property?

Supposing I just pay your rent. Seventy-five sixty-three a month, isn't it?

CORIE Ha-ha . . .

PAUL And you can have the furniture and the wedding gifts. I'd just like to keep my clothes.

CORIE (*Shocked, she turns to* PAUL) I hardly expected bitterness from you.

PAUL I'm not bitter. That's a statement of fact. You're always wearing my pajamas and slippers.

CORIE Only after you go to work.

PAUL Why?

CORIE Because I like the way they—never mind. It's stupid. (*She begins to sob, gets up and goes up the steps to the bedroom*) I'll sign over your pajamas and slippers.

PAUL If you'd like, you can visit them once a month.

CORIE (*Turns back on the landing*) That's bitter!

PAUL You're damned right it is.

CORIE (*Beginning to cry in earnest*) You have no right to be bitter.

PAUL Don't tell me when to be bitter.

CORIE Things just didn't work out.

PAUL They sure as hell didn't.

CORIE You can't say we didn't try.

PAUL Almost two whole weeks.

CORIE It's better than finding out in two *years.*

PAUL Or twenty.

CORIE Or fifty.

PAUL Lucky, aren't we?

CORIE We're the luckiest people in the whole world.

PAUL I thought you weren't going to cry.

CORIE Well, I am! I'm going to have the biggest cry I ever had in my life. And I'm going to enjoy it. (PAUL *drops the pencil and pad into the attaché case, and buries his head in a pillow from the couch*) Because I'm going to cry so loud, I'm going to keep you awake all night long. Good night, Paul! . . . I mean, *good-bye!* (*She goes into the bedroom and slams the door, and we hear her crying.* PAUL *angrily slams his attaché case shut, gets up, and moves toward the stairs. At this moment, the bedroom door opens and* CORIE *throws out a blanket, sheet, and pillow which land at* PAUL's *feet. Then she slams the door shut again. Again we hear crying from the bedroom.* PAUL *picks them up and glares at the door*)

PAUL (*Mimicking* CORIE) . . . all night long . . . work like a dog for a lousy six cents . . . (*Seething,* PAUL *throws the bedding on the end table, and begins to try to make up the sofa with the sheet and blanket, all the while mumbling through the whole argument they have just had. As he puts the blanket over the sofa, he suddenly bursts out)* . . . Six days does not a week make.

(The phone rings. For a moment, PAUL *attempts to ignore it, but it keeps on ringing and he finally storms over to it and rips the cord from the wall. Then, still mumbling to himself, he crosses to the light switch near the door and shuts off the lights. Moonlight from the skylight falls onto the sofa.* PAUL *gets into his makeshift bed and finally settles down. And then . . . it begins to snow. Through the hole in the skylight it falls, down onto* PAUL's *exposed head. He feels it and, after a quick moment, rises up on his knees and looks up at the hole. Soundlessly, he crumples into a heap)*

Curtain

Act Three

ACT THREE

The following day. About 5:00 P.M.

CORIE is at the couch picking up the towels she has put down on the floor and the arm of the couch to soak up the water left by the previous night's snow. She picks up the towels with great distaste and uses one to rub off the arm. She looks up at the hole in the skylight, rolls the couch downstage so that it will not be under the skylight, and takes the towels up into the bathroom. As she disappears into the bathroom, the front door opens and PAUL comes in, collapsing over the railing. He looks haggard and drawn, not just from the stairs, but from a lack of sleep and peace of mind. Also, he has a cold, and as he leans there, he wearily blows his nose. He carries his attaché case and a newspaper. The doorbell buzzes, and as he presses the buzzer, CORIE comes out of the bathroom. They look silently at one another and then they both move, crossing each other wordlessly; PAUL goes up the steps to the bedroom and CORIE crosses up to the kitchen. Just before he gets to the bedroom door, PAUL sneezes.

CORIE (*About to go behind the screen, coldly, without looking at him*) God bless him!

    (*PAUL goes into the bedroom and slams the door. CORIE goes into the kitchen. She comes out with two plates, two knives and forks, and a napkin. Crossing to the table under the radiator, she puts down a plate with a knife and fork. Then putting the other setting down on the end table, she moves it all the way to the other side of the room. She goes back into the kitchen and emerges with two glasses. One she places on the side table and as she crosses toward the other table, our old friend Harry Pepper the* TELEPHONE MAN, *appears at the door. He is breathing as hard as ever. She sees him)*

CORIE Oh, hi!

TELEPHONE MAN (*Not too thrilled*) Hello again.

CORIE How have you been?

TELEPHONE MAN Fine. Fine, thanks.

CORIE Good . . . The telephone's out of order.

TELEPHONE MAN I know. I wouldn't be here for a social call.

CORIE Come on in . . .
(*He steps up into the apartment.* CORIE *closes the door behind him, and goes up into the kitchen to fill her glass with water*)

TELEPHONE MAN (*Looking around*) Hey! . . . Not bad . . . Not bad at all . . . you did a very nice job.

CORIE (*Speaking from the kitchen*) Thanks. You know anyone who might want to rent it?

TELEPHONE MAN You movin' *already?*

CORIE (*Picking up the salt and pepper shakers*) I'm looking for a smaller place.

TELEPHONE MAN (*Looks around with disbelief*) Smaller than this? . . . They're not easy to find.

CORIE (*Coming out of the kitchen*) I'll find one.
(*She places the glass of water and the shakers on the end table*)

TELEPHONE MAN (*Moves to the phone*) Well, let's see what the trouble is. (*The* TELEPHONE MAN *picks up the receiver, jiggles the buttons, and listens, while* CORIE *moves the straight-backed bentwood chair to back of the end table. He puts down the receiver*) It's dead.

CORIE I know. My husband killed it.
(*She crosses to the side table under the radiator, and takes a candlestick and candle, and a small vase with a yellow rose*)

TELEPHONE MAN (*Puzzled*) Oh! (*He looks down and notices that the wire has been pulled from the wall. He kneels down, opens his tool box, and cheerfully begins to replace the wire*) So how do you like married life?

CORIE (*Puts the candlestick and vase down on her table; blandly*) Very interesting.
(*She goes up into the kitchen*)

TELEPHONE MAN Well, after a couple of weeks, what's not interesting? Yeah, it's always nice to see two young kids getting started. With all the trouble today, you see a couple of newlyweds, you figure there's still hope for the world. (*As* CORIE *comes out of the kitchen with a pot of food, a ladle, and a pot holder,* PAUL, *still in his overcoat and with his attaché case and newspaper, comes out of the bedroom and slams the door behind him. Both* CORIE and the TELEPHONE MAN stop. PAUL goes into the bathroom and slams that door hard. CORIE grimaces and the TELEPHONE MAN is shocked. Puzzled) Who's that?

CORIE (Rising above it) Him!

TELEPHONE MAN Your husband?

CORIE (Going to the bathroom door) I suppose so. I wasn't looking. (She pounds on the door with the ladle, and yells) Dinnah—is served!
(She crosses to the side table and begins to ladle food onto the plate. The bathroom door opens, and PAUL comes out)

PAUL (Nods at the TELEPHONE MAN and then moves down the stairs to the couch) I have my own dinner, thank you.
(He sits on the couch, puts his attaché case on the table, and opens it)

CORIE (Ignoring PAUL, crosses to the TELEPHONE MAN and offers him the plate) . . . Would you like some goulash?

TELEPHONE MAN (Embarrassed, he looks at PAUL) Er, no, thanks. We're not allowed to accept tips. (He laughs at his small joke. CORIE takes the plate to the kitchen and drops the goulash, plate and all, into the garbage can. She then moves to her table and ladles goulash onto her plate. PAUL, meantime, has taken a small bag out of his attaché case. It contains a small bunch of grapes which he carefully places on top of his case. CORIE places the pot on the floor, and taking a book of matches from her apron pocket, she lights the candle. While she does

this she sings to herself . . . *"Shama, shama"* . . . PAUL
buries himself in his paper and begins to eat his grapes.

TELEPHONE MAN (*Taking all this in*) I'll be out of here
as fast as I can.
(*He dives back to his work*)

CORIE (*Sitting down to eat*) Take your time. No one's
rushing you.
(*The* TELEPHONE MAN *begins a nervous, tuneless
hum as he works.* PAUL *continues to eat and read
wordlessly. There is a long pause*)

PAUL (*Without looking up*) Is there any beer in the
house? (CORIE *does not answer. The* TELEPHONE MAN
stops humming and looks at her, hoping she will . . .
There is a pause . . . PAUL *is still looking at his newspaper*) I said, is there any beer in the house?
(*There is no answer*)

TELEPHONE MAN (*He can't stand it any longer*) Would
you like me to look?

CORIE There is *no* beer in the house.
(PAUL *throws down his paper and storms toward
the* TELEPHONE MAN, *who draws back in fright.*
PAUL *stops at the bar and pours himself a drink*)

TELEPHONE MAN (*With great relief, and trying to make
conversation because no one else will*) That's my trouble . . . beer . . . I can drink ten cans in a night . . . of
beer.
(PAUL *goes back to the couch and his newspaper.
Not having eased the tension any, the* TELEPHONE
MAN *goes back to his work and again begins his
nervous humming*)

113

PAUL (*After another pause, still looking at his newspaper*)
Did my laundry come back today?

CORIE (*With food in her mouth, she takes her own sweet
time in answering*) Hmph.

PAUL (*Looks at her*) What does that mean?

CORIE It meant your laundry came back today . . . They
stuffed your shirts beautifully.
(*Having watched this exchange, the* TELEPHONE
MAN *desperately begins to whistle a pointless and
innocuous tune*)

PAUL (*Stung, takes a drink, then becoming aware of the*
TELEPHONE MAN) Would you like a drink? (*There is
no answer. The* TELEPHONE MAN *continues to work*)
I said, would you like a drink?

TELEPHONE MAN (*Startled, he looks up from his work*)
Who?

PAUL You!

TELEPHONE MAN Me?

PAUL Yes!

TELEPHONE MAN OH! . . . NO!

PAUL Right.
(*He goes back to his newspaper*)

TELEPHONE MAN (*Dives back to his work*) One more
little screw should do it . . . There! (*Turns the screw,*

then says loud and elatedly) I'm finished! I'm finished! (*He throws the tools quickly back into his kit*) That wasn't too long, was it?

CORIE   No. Thank you very much.

TELEPHONE MAN (*Getting up and crossing to the door*) It's A. T. and T.'s pleasure.
(*He nearly drops the kit, and in a panic rushes to the door. He is anxious to leave this scene*)

CORIE (*Picks up the pot from the floor and moves to him at the door*) I'm sorry to keep bothering you like this.

TELEPHONE MAN   Oh, listen. Anytime.

CORIE (*Very confidingly*)   I don't think we'll be needing you again.

TELEPHONE MAN   Well, I wouldn't be too sure . . . Phones keep breaking down now and then but er . . . (*He looks at* CORIE *as if trying to get some secret and personal message across to cheer her up*) . . . somehow, they have a way of getting fixed. You know what I mean . . . (*He winks at her to indicate "Chin up." As he's winking,* PAUL *lowers his paper, turns around, and sees him. The* TELEPHONE MAN *is terribly embarrassed. So he winks at* PAUL. *Then, pulling himself together*) Well . . . 'bye.
(*And he rushes out of the door.* CORIE *closes the door behind him and goes up into the kitchen with the pot and ladle. As soon as she is safely behind the screen,* PAUL *puts down his paper and runs to her table, where he swipes a mouthful of goulash. Dashing back to the couch, he is once more hidden*

behind his newspaper when CORIE *comes out of the kitchen. She is now carrying a plate on which rests a small iced cake. She sits down, and pushing her plate aside, begins to eat her cake)*

CORIE   Are you going to stay here again tonight?

PAUL   I haven't found a room yet.

CORIE   You've had all day to look.

PAUL   (*Using the nasal spray he had taken out of the attaché case with the bag of grapes*)   I've been very busy. I work during the day, you know.

CORIE   You could look during your lunch hour.

PAUL   I *eat* during my lunch hour. I'll look during my looking hour.
    (*He puts down the spray and takes another drink*)

CORIE   You could look tonight.

PAUL   I intended to. (*He goes back to reading his paper*) But I'm coming down with a cold. I thought I'd just take a couple of aspirins and get right into the sofa.

CORIE   I'm sure you can find *some* place . . . Why don't you sleep at your club?

PAUL   It's not *that* kind of a club. It's a locker room and a handball court . . . and to sleep there I'd have to keep winning the serve. (*He looks at* CORIE) Look, does it bother you if I stay here another couple of days?

CORIE It's your apartment, too. Get out whenever you
want to get out. (*The phone rings. When* PAUL *makes
no move to answer it,* CORIE, *with great resignation,
crosses to the phone and picks it up*) Hello? . . . Who?
. . . Yes, it is. (CORIE *suddenly acts very feminine, in a
somewhat lower, more provocative and confidential
voice, even laughing at times as though she were sharing
some private little joke. She seems to be doing this all
for* PAUL's *benefit. Into the phone*) . . . Oh, isn't that
nice . . . Yes, I'm very interested . . . (*Takes the phone
and moves away from* PAUL) Thursday night? . . .
Well, I don't see why not . . .

PAUL (*Doesn't like the sound of this*) Who is that?

CORIE (*Ignores him and laughs into the phone*) . . .
What's that? . . . Eight o'clock? . . . It sounds perfect.

PAUL Who are you talking to?

CORIE (*Still ignoring him*) . . . I see . . . But how did
you get my number? . . . Oh, isn't that clever . . .

PAUL (*Crosses angrily and grabs the receiver*) Give me
that phone.

CORIE (*Struggling with him for it*) I will not. Get away
from here, Paul. It's for me.

PAUL I said give me that phone. (*Takes the receiver and
its cradle from her.* CORIE *storms across to her table with
great indignation, blows the candle out, and begins to
take her setting into the kitchen.* PAUL, *into the phone*)
Hello? . . . Who is this? . . . Who? . . . (*He looks*

at CORIE *incredulously)* No, madam, we're *not* interested in Bossa Nova lessons. (PAUL *hangs up and stares at* CORIE *as she comes out of the kitchen.* CORIE *does not look at him as she finishes clearing the table and takes the plates into the kitchen.* PAUL *moves back to the couch and sits)* I'm glad we didn't have children . . . because you're a crazy lady.

CORIE (*Moves the chair back to the right, and carries the table back to the right of the couch*) I'll go where I want and do what I want. And I'm not going to stay in this house at nights as long as you're here.

PAUL (*Putting down the paper*) I see . . . Okay, Corie, when do you want me out?

CORIE I want you out now. Tonight.

PAUL (*Crossing to the closet*) Okay! Fine! (*He gets his suitcase and puts it on top of the end table*) I'll be out of here in five minutes. Is that soon enough for you?

CORIE Not if you can make it in two.

PAUL (*Opening the suitcase*) You can't wait, can you? You just can't wait till I'm gone and out of your life.

CORIE Right. When do I get it?

PAUL Get what?

CORIE My divorce. When do I get my divorce?

PAUL How should I know? They didn't even send us our marriage license yet.

CORIE I'll get your Jockey shorts.
(*She goes up into the bedroom*)

PAUL (*Moves to the coffee table and takes his drink*) You can leave the suits. I'll pick them up in the spring when they're dry.

CORIE (*In the bedroom*) You'd better ring the bell. 'Cause I'm buying a big dog tomorrow.

PAUL (*Finishing his drink*) A dog . . . Fine, fine . . . Now you'll have someone to walk barefoot in the park with. (*The phone rings.* CORIE *comes out of the bedroom with a pile of Jockey shorts which she throws on the couch. She crosses to answer the phone*) If that's Arthur Murray, say hello.
        (*He gathers up the Jockey shorts and puts them in the suitcase*)

CORIE (*Picks up the phone*) Hello . . . Yes, Aunt Harriet . . . What? . . . No, mother's not with me . . . I'm positive . . . She left about two in the morning . . . What's wrong? . . . *What?*

PAUL (*Crossing to the closet and getting a pair of pants*) What is it?

CORIE (*Terribly   frightened*) Mother??? . . . My Mother??? . . . Are you *sure?*

PAUL (*Putting the pants in the suitcase*) What is it?

CORIE (*Into the phone, now very nervous*) No, my phone's been out of order all day . . . (*She gives* PAUL *a dirty look)* No, I don't know *what* could have happened.

PAUL *(Blowing his nose)* What's the matter.

CORIE All right, Aunt Harriet, don't get excited . . . Yes . . . Yes, I'll call as soon as I hear.
(She hangs up)

PAUL *(Moves to* CORIE*)* What happened to your mother?

CORIE She didn't come home last night. Her bed wasn't slept in. Maybe I should call the police.
(She starts to pick up the phone)

PAUL All right, take it easy, Corie . . .

CORIE *(Turns back to* PAUL*)* Don't you understand? Jessie looked. She was not in her bedroom this morning.
(She picks up the phone)

PAUL *(Groping)* Well . . . well, maybe her back was bothering her and she went to sleep on the ironing board.

CORIE You stupid idiot, didn't you hear what I said? My mother's been missing all night! . . . *My* mother!

PAUL *(The Chief of Police)* All right, let's not crack up.

CORIE *(Seething)* Will you go 'way. Get out of my life and go away! *(She slams the receiver down and crosses to the door)* I don't want to see you here when I get back.

PAUL   Where are you going?

CORIE   Upstairs to find out what happened to my mother. (*She opens the door*) And don't be here when I get back!
(*She goes out and slams the door.* PAUL *goes to the door*)

PAUL   Oh, yeah? . . . Well, I've got a big surprise for you . . . (*He opens the door and yells after her*) I'm not going to be here when you get back . . . (*Crossing to the dictionary on the side table*) Let's see how you like living alone . . . (*He pulls ties out of the dictionary and throws them in the suitcase*) A dog . . . Ha! That's a laugh . . . Wait till she tries to take him out for a walk . . . He'll get one look at those stairs and he'll go right for her throat. (*Crossing into the bedroom*) You might as well get a parakeet, too . . . So you can talk to him all night. (*Mimicking* CORIE) "How much can I spend for bird seeds, Polly? Is a nickel too much?" (*He comes out of the bedroom with shirts and pajamas*) Well, fortunately, I don't need anyone to protect me. (*Putting the clothes in the suitcase*) Because I am a man, sweetheart . . . An independent, mature, self-sufficient man. (*He sneezes as he closes the suitcase*) God bless me! (*Feeling sorry for himself, he feels his head*) I probably got the flu. (*Crossing to the bar, he takes a bottle and glass*) Yeah, I'm hot, cold, sweating, freezing. It's probably a twenty-four-hour virus. I'll be all right . . . (*He looks at his watch*) . . . tomorrow at a quarter to five. (*He pours another drink, puts down the bottle, and drinks. As he drinks, he notices the hole in the skylight. Stepping up onto the black leather armchair*) Oh! . . . Oh, thanks a lot, pal. (*He holds the glass up in toast fashion*) "And thus it was written, some shall die by pestilence, some by the plague . . . and one poor schnook is gonna get it from a hole in the ceiling." (*Getting down, he puts the drink on the side table*) Well, I guess that's it. (*He gets the bottle of Scotch from the bar, and glances at the bedroom*) Good-bye, leaky closet . . . (*To the bathroom*) Good-bye, no bathtub . . . (*Taking the attaché case from the coffee table, he looks up at the hole*) Good-bye, hole . . . (*Getting his suitcase*) Good-bye, six flights . . . (*As* PAUL *moves to the door,* CORIE *comes in. She holds her apron to her mouth, and is very disturbed*) Good-bye, Corie . . . (PAUL *stops in the doorway as* CORIE *wordlessly goes right by him and starts to go up the stairs to the bedroom*) Don't I get a good-bye? . . . According to law, I'm entitled to a good-bye!

CORIE (*Stops on the stairs and slowly turns back to* PAUL, *in a heart-rending wail*) Good-bye . . .
(*She goes into the bedroom and collapses on the bed*)

PAUL   Corie . . . Now what is it? (*Alarmed, he drops the suitcase and attaché case, and puts the bottle on the end table*) Is it your mother? . . . Was it an accident? . . . (*He crosses to the bedroom*) Corie, for pete's sakes, what happened to your mother?
(*Suddenly* MOTHER *rushes in through the open door. She is now dressed in a man's bathrobe many sizes too big for her. Over-sized man's slippers flap on her bare feet. But she is holding her pocketbook. Desperately clutching the bathrobe, she crosses to the bedroom*)

MOTHER   Corie, please, listen! . . . It's not the way it looks at all!

PAUL (*Looks at her in amazement*) Mother???

MOTHER (*Stops momentarily*) Oh, good morning, Paul. (*She goes up the stairs*) Corie, you've got to talk to me. (CORIE *slams the door to the bedroom shut*) There's a perfectly good explanation. (*Hysterical, in front of the closed door*) Corie, please . . . You're not being fair . . . (*She turns to* PAUL) Paul, make her believe me.

PAUL (*Goes up the stairs and pounds on the bedroom door*) Now, you see . . . Now are you satisfied? . . . (*He turns to* MOTHER, *being very forgiving*) It's all right, Mother, I understand.
(*He starts for his suitcase*)

MOTHER (*Shocked*) No! . . . You don't understand!!! (*She goes to* PAUL) You don't understand at all!! . . .

PAUL (*Picking up the suitcase, attaché case, and bottle*) As long as you're all right, Mother.
(*He looks at her, sadly shakes his head and exits*)

MOTHER (*Trying to stop him*) No, Paul . . . You've got to believe me . . . (*But* PAUL *is gone*) Oh, this is awful . . . Somebody believe me.
(*The bedroom door opens and* CORIE *comes out*)

CORIE Paul! Where's Paul? . . .

MOTHER (*Putting her bag down on the end table*) Corie, I'm going to explain everything. The bathrobe, the slippers . . . It's all just a big mistake.

CORIE (*Rushing to the front door*) Did he go? Did Paul leave?

MOTHER (*Going to* CORIE) It happened last night . . . when I left with Mr. Velasco . . .

CORIE (*Closing the door*) He was right . . . Paul was right.
(*She moves to the couch and sits*)

MOTHER (*Following her*) It must have been the drinks. I had a great deal to drink last night . . . (*She sits next to* CORIE) I had Scotch, martinis, coffee, black bean soup, and Uzus . . .

CORIE You don't have to explain a thing to me, Mother.

MOTHER (*Horrified*) But I want to explain . . . When I got outside I suddenly felt dizzy . . . and I fainted . . . Well, I passed out. In the slush.

CORIE I should have listened to him . . . It's all my fault.

MOTHER (*Desperately trying to make her see*) Then Victor picked me up and carried me inside. I couldn't walk because my shoes fell down the sewer.

CORIE (*Deep in her own misery*) You hear about these things every day.

MOTHER He started to carry me up here but his beret fell over his eyes, and he fell down the stairs . . . He fell into apartment Three-C. I fell on his foot . . . They had to carry us up.

CORIE I thought we'd have a nice sociable evening, that's all.

MOTHER . . . Mr. Gonzales, Mr. Armandariz, and Mr. Calhoun . . . (*She sags in defeat*) They carried us up . . .

CORIE Just some drinks, dinner, and coffee . . . That's all . . .

MOTHER And then they put us down. On the rugs . . . Oh, he doesn't have beds . . . just thick rugs, and then I fell asleep . . .

CORIE Paul was right. He was right about so many things . . .

MOTHER And then when I woke up, Victor was gone. But I was there . . . in his bathrobe. (*She pounds the couch with her fist*) I swear that's the truth, Corie.

CORIE (*Turns to* MOTHER) You don't have to swear, Mother.

MOTHER But I want you to believe me. I've told you everything.

CORIE Then where are your clothes?

MOTHER *That* I can't tell you.

CORIE Why not?

MOTHER Because you won't believe me.

CORIE I'll believe you.

MOTHER You won't.

CORIE I will. Where are your clothes?

MOTHER I don't know.

CORIE I don't believe you.
(*She gets up and moves toward* MOTHER)

MOTHER Didn't I say you wouldn't believe me? I just
don't know where they are . . . (*She gets up and moves
to the right*) Oh, Corie, I've never been so humiliated
in all my life . . .

CORIE Don't blame yourself . . . It's all my fault. *I* did it.
I did this to you.
(*She leans on the bar, holding her head*)

MOTHER And I had horrible nightmares. I dreamt my
fingers were falling off because I couldn't make a fist.
(*She paces and catches sight of herself in the mirror*)
Oh, God! I look like someone they woke up in the middle of the night on the *Andrea Doria!*
(*She breaks into hysterical laughter, and then there
is a pounding on the door*)

VELASCO'S VOICE Hello. Anyone home? . . .

MOTHER (*Terror-stricken*) It's him . . . (*She rushes to*
CORIE) Corie, don't let him in. I can't face him now . . .
not in his bathrobe.
(*There is another pounding at the door*)

VELASCO'S VOICE Somebody, please!

CORIE (*Moving past* MOTHER) All right, Mother. I'll han-
dle this. Go in the bedroom . . .

MOTHER (*Moving to the stairs*) Tell him I'm not here. Tell him anything.

>(*The door opens and* VELASCO *steps in. He is now supporting himself with a cane and his foot is covered by a thick white stocking. As* VELASCO *enters,* CORIE *sinks into the armchair at right of the couch*)

VELASCO (*Hobbling up the step and moving to the couch*) I'm sorry but I need some aspirins desperately. (*He catches sight of* MOTHER *who is furtively trying to escape up the stairs to the bedroom*) Hello, Ethel.

MOTHER (*Caught, she stops and tries to cover her embarrassment*) Oh, hello, Victor . . . Mr. Victor . . . Mr. Velasco.

VELASCO (*To* CORIE) Did you hear what happened to us last night? (*To* MOTHER) Did you tell her what happened to us last night?

MOTHER (*Horrified*) Why . . . ? What happened to us last night? (*She composes herself*) Oh, you mean what happened to us last night. (*With great nonchalance, moving down the stairs*) Yes . . . Yes . . . I told her.

VELASCO (*At the couch*) Did you know my big toe is broken?

MOTHER (*Smiles*) Yes . . . (*She catches herself*) I mean no . . . Isn't that terrible?

VELASCO I'll have to wear a slipper for the next month . . . Only I can't find my slippers . . . (*He sees them on* MOTHER'*s feet*) Oh, there they are . . .

MOTHER (*Looks down at her feet, as if surprised*) Oh, yes . . . There's your slippers.

VELASCO (*Sitting on the sofa and putting his foot up on the coffee table*) It took me forty minutes to walk up the stairs . . . I'll have to hire someone to pull me up the ladder. (*To* CORIE) Corie, could I please have about three hundred aspirins?
(CORIE *crosses to the stairs*)

MOTHER (*Appealing to* CORIE) A broken toe . . . Isn't that awful!
(CORIE *ignores her and goes into the bathroom*)

VELASCO That's not the worst of it. I just had a complete examination. Guess what else I have?

MOTHER What?

VELASCO An ulcer! From all the rich food . . . I have to take little pink pills like you.

MOTHER Oh, dear . . .

VELASCO You know something, Ethel . . . I don't think I'm as young as I think I am.

MOTHER Why do you say that?

VELASCO Isn't it obvious? Last night I couldn't carry you up the stairs. I can't eat rich foods any more . . . (*Very confidentially*) . . . and I dye my hair.

MOTHER (*Moves to the couch*) Oh . . . Well, it looks very nice.

VELASCO Thank you . . . So are you . . .

MOTHER (*Sitting next to* VELASCO) Oh . . . Thank you.

VELASCO I mean it, Ethel. You're a very unusual woman.

MOTHER Unusual? . . . In what way?

VELASCO (*Reflectively*) It's funny, but I can hardly feel my big toe at all now.

MOTHER (*Insistent*) Unusual in what way?

VELASCO Well, I took a look at you last night . . . I took a long, close look at you . . . Do you know what you are, Ethel?

MOTHER (*Ready for the compliment*) What?

VELASCO A good sport.

MOTHER Oh . . . A good sport.

VELASCO To have gone through all you did last night. The trip to Staten Island, the strange food, the drinks, being carried up to my apartment like that. And you didn't say one word about it.

MOTHER Well, I didn't have much chance to . . . I did a lot of fainting.

VELASCO Yes . . . As a matter of fact, we both did . . . If you remember . . .
(*Remembering, he begins to laugh*)

MOTHER Yes . . . (*She joins in. It is a warm, hearty laugh shared by two friends. After the laugh gradually dies out, there is a moment of awkward silence and then with an attempt at renewed gaiety,* MOTHER *says)* Mr. Velasco . . . Where are my clothes?

VELASCO   Your clothes . . . ? Oh, yes . . . *(He takes a piece of paper out of his pocket)* Here.
(He gives it to her)

MOTHER   I'm sure I wore more than that.

VELASCO   It's a cleaning ticket. They're sending them up at six o'clock.

MOTHER *(Taking the ticket)*   Oh, they're at the cleaner's . . . *(After a moment's hesitation)* When did I take them off?

VELASCO   You didn't . . . You were drenched and out cold. Gonzales took them off.

MOTHER *(Shocked)*   Mr. Gonzales??

VELASCO   Not Mister! . . . *Doctor* Gonzales!

MOTHER *(Relieved)*   Doctor . . . Oh, *Doctor* Gonzales . . . Well, I suppose that's all right. How convenient to have an M.D. in the building.

VELASCO *(Laughing)*   He's not an M.D. He's a Doctor of Philosophy.

MOTHER *(Joins in the laughter with great abandon)*   Oh, no . . .
*(*CORIE *comes out of the bathroom with aspirin and*

*a glass of water, and watches them laughing with
bewilderment)*

CORIE *(Goes behind the couch)* Here's the aspirins.

VELASCO Thank you, but I'm feeling better now.

MOTHER *I'll* take them.
(*Takes an aspirin and a sip of water*)

VELASCO *(Gets up and hobbles to the door)* I have to go.
I'm supposed to soak my foot every hour . . .

MOTHER Oh, dear . . . Is there anything I can do?

VELASCO *(Turns back)* Yes . . . Yes, there is . . . Would
you like to have dinner with me tonight?

MOTHER *(Surprised)* Me?

VELASCO *(Nods)* If you don't mind eating plain food.

MOTHER I love *plain* food.

VELASCO Good . . . I'll call the New York Hospital for a
reservation . . . (*He opens the door*) Pick me up in a
few minutes . . . We'll have a glass of buttermilk before
we go.
(*He exits*)

MOTHER *(After a moment, she turns to* CORIE *on the stairs
and giggles. Takes the grapes from the coffee table*)
You know what? . . . I'll bet I'm the first woman ever
asked to dinner wearing a size forty-eight bathrobe.

CORIE (*Lost in her own problem*) Mother, can I talk to you for a minute?

MOTHER (*Puts down the bunch of grapes, gets up, and moves right*) I just realized. I slept without a board . . . For the first time in years I slept without a board.

CORIE Mother, will you listen . . .

MOTHER (*Turns to* CORIE) You don't suppose Uzu is a Greek miracle drug, do you?
(*She flips a grape back and forth and pops it into her mouth like a knichi*)

CORIE Mother, before you go, there's something we've got to talk about.

MOTHER (*Moving to* CORIE) Oh, Corie, how sweet . . . You're worried about me.

CORIE I am *not* worried about you.

MOTHER (*Looks in the mirror*) Oh, dear. My hair. What am I going to do with my hair?

CORIE I don't *care* what you do with your hair.

MOTHER If *he* can dye it, why can't I? Do you think black would make me look too Mexican?

CORIE Mother, why won't you talk to me?

MOTHER (*Moving back of the couch*) Now? . . . But Victor's waiting . . . (*She turns back to* CORIE) Why don't you and Paul come with us?

CORIE That's what I've been trying to tell you . . . Paul isn't coming back.

MOTHER What do you mean? Where'd he go?

CORIE I don't know. Reno. Texas. Wherever it is that men go to get divorced.

MOTHER *Divorced???*

CORIE That's right. Divorced. Paul and I have split up. For good.

MOTHER I don't believe it.

CORIE Why don't you believe it?

MOTHER You? And Paul?

CORIE Well, you just saw him leave here with his suitcase. What did you think he had in there?

MOTHER I don't know. I know how neat he is. I thought maybe the garbage.

CORIE Mother, I believe *you*. Why won't you believe me?

MOTHER (*Moves left to the bentwood chair and sits facing* CORIE) Because in my entire life I've never seen two people more in love than you and Paul.

CORIE (*Tearfully*) Well, it's not true. It may have been yesterday but it sure isn't today. It's all over, Mother. He's gone.

133

MOTHER You mean he just walked out? For no reason at all? . . .

CORIE He had a perfectly *good* reason. I *told* him to get out. *I* did it. Me and my big stupid mouth.

MOTHER It couldn't have been all your fault.

CORIE No? . . . No?? Because of me you're running around without your clothes and Paul is out there on the streets with a cold looking for a place to sleep. Who's fault is that?

MOTHER Yours! . . . But do you want to know something that may shock you? . . . I still love you.

CORIE You do? . . .

MOTHER Yes, and Paul loves you, too.

CORIE And I love him . . . Only I don't know what he wants. I don't know how to make him happy . . . Oh, Mom, what am I going to do?

MOTHER That's the first time you've asked my advice since you were ten. (*She gets up and moves to* CORIE) It's very simple. You've just got to give up a little of you for him. Don't make everything a game. Just late at night in that little room upstairs. But take care of him. And make him feel important. And if you can do that, you'll have a happy and wonderful marriage . . . Like two out of every ten couples . . . But you'll be one of the two, baby . . . (*She gently strokes* CORIE's *hair*) Now get your coat and go on out after him . . . I've got a date. (*She crosses to the coffee table and picks up her*

handbag) Aunt Harriet isn't going to believe a word of this . . . *(Flourishing her bathrobe, she moves to the door and opens it)* I wish I had my Polaroid camera . . .
(She pauses, blows CORIE *a kiss, and exits.* CORIE *thinks a moment, wipes her eyes, and then rushes to the closet for her coat. Without stopping to put it on, she rushes to the door and opens it. As the door opens,* PAUL *is revealed at the doorway. He greets* CORIE *with a loud sneeze. His clothes are disheveled, his overcoat is gone, and he is obviously drunk, but he still is carrying his suitcase)*

CORIE Paul! . . . Paul, are you all right? . . .

PAUL *(Very carefully crossing to the coffee table)* Fine . . . Fine, thank you . . .
(He giggles)

CORIE *(Moves to him)* I was just going out to look for you.

PAUL *(Puts the suitcase on the floor and starts to take out his clothes)* Oh . . . ? Where were you going to look? . . .

CORIE I don't know. I was just going to look.

PAUL *(Confidentially)* Oh . . . ! Well, you'll never find me.
(He throws a handful of clothes into the closet. He is apparently amused by some secret joke)

CORIE Paul, I've got so much to say to you, darling.

PAUL *(Taking more clothes out of the suitcase)* So,

have I, Corie . . . I got all the way downstairs and suddenly it hit me. I saw everything clearly for the first time. (*He moves up left to behind the couch*) I said to myself, this is crazy . . . Crazy! . . . It's all wrong for me to run like this . . . (*He turns to* CORIE) And there's only one right thing to do, Corie.

CORIE (*Moving to him*) Really, Paul? . . . What? . . .

PAUL (*Jubilantly*) *You* get out!
(*He breaks into hysterical laughter*)

CORIE What? . . .

PAUL Why should I get out? I'm paying a hundred twenty-five a month . . . (*He looks about the apartment*) . . . for this . . . You get out.
(*He stuffs clothes into the dictionary*)

CORIE But I don't want to get out!

PAUL (*Crossing back to the suitcase and getting another handful of clothes*) I'm afraid you'll have to . . . The lease is in my name . . . (*He moves to the stairs*) I'll give you ten minutes to pack your goulash.

CORIE (*Moves to him*) Paul, your coat! . . . Where is your coat?

PAUL (*Draws himself up in indignation*) Coat? . . . I don't need a coat . . . It's only two degrees . . .
(*He starts to go up the stairs, slips and falls*)

CORIE (*Rushing to him*) Paul, are you all right? . . .

PAUL (*Struggling up*) You're dawdling, Corie . . . I want you out of here in exactly ten minutes . . .

CORIE (*Holding him*) Paul, you're ice cold . . . You're freezing! . . . What have you been doing?

PAUL (*Pulls away from her and moves to a chair*) What do you think I've been doing? (*He puts his foot up on the seat*) I've been walking barefoot in the Goddamn park.

CORIE (*Pulls up his pants leg, revealing his stockingless foot*) Where's your socks? . . . Are you crazy?

PAUL No . . . No . . . But guess what I am.

CORIE (*Looks at him*) You're drunk!

PAUL (*In great triumph, he moves right*) Ah . . . ! You finally noticed!!

CORIE Lousy, stinkin' drunk!

PAUL Ah, gee . . . Thanks . . .

CORIE (*Moves to him and feels his forehead*) You're burning up with fever.

PAUL How about that?

CORIE You'll get pneumonia!

PAUL If that's what you want, that is what I'll get.

CORIE (*Leads him to the couch*) I want you to get those

shoes off . . . They're soaking wet . . .
(*She pushes him down onto the couch*)

PAUL I can't . . . My feet have swellened . . .

CORIE (*Pulling his shoes off*) I never should have let
you out of here. I knew you had a cold.
(*She puts the shoes on the side table*)

PAUL (*Getting up and moving to the doorway*) Hey!
Hey, Corie . . . Let's do that thing you said before . . .
Let's wake up the police and see if all the rooms come
out of the crazy neighbors . . . (*He opens the door and
shouts into the hall*) All right, everybody up . . .

CORIE (*Runs to him and pulls him back into the room*)
Will you shut up and get into bed . . . (*As she struggles with him, she tickles him, and* PAUL *falls to the
floor behind the couch.* CORIE *closes the door behind her*)
Get into bed . . .

PAUL You get in first.

CORIE You're sick.

PAUL Not *that* sick . . .
(*He lunges for her and she backs away against the
door*)

CORIE Stop it, Paul . . .

PAUL Come on, Corie. Let's break my fever . . .
(*He grabs her*)

CORIE   I said stop it! (*Struggling to get away*) I mean it, damn you . . . Stop it!
(*She gives him an elbow in the stomach and dodges away through the kitchen*)

PAUL   Gee, you're pretty when you're mean and rotten.

CORIE   Keep away from me, Paul . . . (PAUL *moves toward her*) I'm warning you . . . I'll scream.
(CORIE *keeps the couch between her and* PAUL)

PAUL (*Stops*)   Shh . . . ! There's snow on the roof. We'll have an avalanche! . . .

CORIE (*Dodging behind the chair*)   You shouldn't be walking around like this. You've got a fever . . .

PAUL (*Moving to the chair*)   Stand still! The both of you!

CORIE (*Running up the stairs to the bathroom*)   No, Paul . . . ! I don't like you when you're like this.
(*She barricades herself in the bathroom*)

PAUL (*Chasing her and pounding on the door*)   Open this door!

CORIE (*From the bathroom*)   I can't . . . I'm scared.

PAUL   Of me?

CORIE   Yes.

PAUL   Why?

CORIE Because it's not you anymore . . . I want the old Paul back.

PAUL That fuddy duddy?

CORIE He's not a fuddy duddy. He's dependable and he's strong and he takes care of me and tells me how much I can spend and protects me from people like you . . . (PAUL *suddenly has a brain storm and with great glee sneaks off into the bedroom*) And I just want him to know how much I love him . . . And that I'm going to make everything here exactly the way he wants it . . . I'm going to fix the hole in the skylight . . . and the leak in the closet . . . And I'm going to put in a bathtub and if he wants I'll even carry him up the stairs every night . . . Because I want him to know how much I love him . . . (*Slowly and cautiously opening the door*) Can you hear me, darling? . . . Paul? . . . (PAUL *appears on the skylight. He is crawling drunkenly along the ledge.* CORIE, *having gotten no answer, comes out of the bathroom and goes into the bedroom searching for* PAUL) Paul, are you all right?
    (*She comes out of the bedroom and crosses toward the front door. When she is beneath him,* PAUL *taps on the skylight and stands up.* CORIE, *looking up, sees him and screams*)

CORIE (*Screams*) Paul . . . You idiot . . . Come down . . . You'll kill yourself.

PAUL (*Teetering on the ledge, yelling through the skylight*) I want to be a nut like everyone else in this building.

CORIE (*Up on her knees on the couch, yelling back*) No!

No, Paul! . . . I don't want you to be a nut. I want you to come down.

PAUL   I'll come down when you've said it again . . . Loud and clear.

CORIE   What? . . . Anything, Paul . . . Anything!

PAUL   My husband . . .

CORIE   "My husband . . ."

PAUL   Paul Bratter . . .

CORIE   "Paul Bratter . . ."

PAUL   . . . rising young attorney . . .
    (*He nearly falls off the ledge*)

CORIE   (*Screaming in fright*) ". . . rising young attorney . . ."

PAUL   . . . is a lousy stinkin' drunk . . .

CORIE   ". . . is a lousy stinkin' drunk." . . . And I love him.

PAUL   And I love you, Corie. Even when I didn't like you, I loved you.

CORIE   (*Crossing to* PAUL) Then please, darling . . . Please, come down.

PAUL   I . . . I can't . . . Not now.

CORIE Why not?

PAUL I'm going to be sick . . .
(*He looks around as if to find a place to be sick*)

CORIE Oh, no!

PAUL Oh, yes!

CORIE (*Paces back and forth*) Paul . . . Paul . . . Don't move! I'll come out and get you.

PAUL (*Holding on desperately*) Would you do that, Corie? Because I'm getting panicky!

CORIE Yes . . . Yes, darling, I'm coming . . .
(*She runs off into the bedroom*)

PAUL Corie . . . Corie . . .

CORIE (*Dashing out of the bedroom and down the stairs*) What, Paul? . . . What???

PAUL Don't leave me . . .

CORIE You'll be all right, darling. Just hold on tight. And try to be calm . . .

PAUL How? What should I do?

CORIE (*Ponders*) What should he do? (*To* PAUL) Sing, Paul!

PAUL Sing??

CORIE Sing . . . Keep singing as loud as you can until I come out there. Promise me you'll keep singing, Paul . . .

PAUL Yes, yes . . . I promise . . . I'll keep singing . . .

CORIE (*Moving to the stairs*) But don't stop until I come out . . . I love you, darling . . . Keep singing, Paul . . . Keep singing!
(*She runs off into the bedroom*)

PAUL (*Calling after her in desperation*) Corie, Corie, what song should I sing?? . . . Oh, God . . . (*He pulls himself together*) "Shama, shama. . . ."

Curtain